William Droel

Full-Time Christians

THE REAL CHALLENGE
FROM VATICAN II

TWENTY-THIRD PUBLICATIONS
A Division of Bayard   MYSTIC, CT 06355

Acknowledgments

Thanks to the following for their suggestions on an early draft of this book: Charles DiSalvo, Mary Ann Droel, Maureen Hart, Ed Marciniak, Janet Olson, John Sullivan. Special thanks to Mary Carol Kendzia at Twenty-Third Publications.

Second printing, 2003

Twenty-Third Publications
A Division of Bayard
185 Willow Street
P.O. Box 180
Mystic, CT 06355
(860) 536-2611
(800) 321-0411
www.twentythirdpublications.com

ISBN:1-58595-177-3
Library of Congress Catalog Card Number: 2001135968
Printed in the U.S.A.

Dedication

To Elizabeth and Robert
whom I hope consider it special
to be Chicago Catholics.

Contents

Full-Time Christians

Introduction

I was in high school during the years of the Second Vatican Council. As did most Catholics of that time, I primarily learned about the council through the liturgical changes it brought about. All of these changes appealed to me, and I wanted to take a more active part in what was happening in the church. And so I became a lector, the first lay person in my parish to do so. It was an honor that precipitated my lifelong interest in Scripture study and Scripture-based prayer.

In this same context I first became acquainted with Vatican II's theme of a church-in-the-world. One evening, before Mass, the associate pastor handed me a high school graduation gift: a copy of the book *The Other America,* by Michael Harrington. Although he was once an editor of the Catholic Worker newspaper, Harrington did not write a so-called Catholic book. Yet because a priest gave me the book, I presumed it was for "spiritual reading." The book's association with President John Kennedy, a Catholic icon at that time, also made me think about its connection to my religion.

Vatican II, lectoring at Mass, reading *The Other America;* all of this was new to me. Like any other student in a Catholic school, I contributed nickels to the missions. I participated in food drives and the like during high school. But never before was I aware that someone's spiritual life could be enhanced by combating poverty through a career in social work or in government. It wasn't very clear to me then, but all of this was my first inkling of what the post-Vatican II church was supposed to be.

At about the same time there was a race riot in Rochester, New York, where I lived at the time. I was impressed that in the wake of the riot, the churches—mostly Protestant—raised money, not to reconstruct the vandalized buildings or to compensate victims of the riots, but to hire Saul Alinsky of Chicago, Illinois, to form a community organization that was intended to help African-Americans participate in the economy and political life of Rochester. In subsequent months, I was impressed by the effectiveness of Alinsky and his colleagues in starting up this organization, which came to be known as FIGHT (for Freedom, Integration, God, Honor, Today).

Was there a way, I wondered, that I could connect my budding interest in public policy and race relations to my strong commitment to the Catholic faith? I went back and read the documents of Vatican II. I also went to a used bookstore and found some old textbooks based on the social encyclicals of 1891 and 1931. The examples used in those texts and in other materials were often from Chicago: the Christian Family Movement, the Catholic Labor Alliance, the Young Christian Workers and Young Christian Students, the monthly newspaper *Work*, the Catholic Interracial Council, the Cana Conference, St. Benet's Bookshop, the Adult Education Centers, the Office of Urban Affairs, and Saul Alinsky's Industrial Areas Foundation. And so I eventually concluded that it would be necessary for me to move to Chicago if I was to make a strong connection between my Catholic heritage and my interest in society.

Ironically, when I arrived in Chicago, I learned that Alinsky's Industrial Areas Foundation—the group with which I was most familiar—had just moved its headquarters to Long Island, New York. IAF has since moved back to Chicago. Another contact I had hoped to make was with Msgr. John Egan of Chicago, Alinsky's friend and a Catholic activist whom I had previously met. I learned that he too had moved out of state.

Within a few months, however, I met Russell Barta of Mundelein College and, through him, Msgr. Daniel Cantwell, Ed Marciniak, and others associated with the Chicago Declaration of Christian Concern. I discovered that they, too, sought a connection between their faith and improving the world in which we live.

As a result of those friendships, as well as through involvement in numerous projects over these past thirty years, I have deepened my appreciation for the vision of Vatican II. This book will explain that vision in a North American context and will point to opportunities that await Christians who take up the challenges of the Second Vatican Council.

This book is not just for Catholics. There is no patent on the message of Vatican II. Its themes can be adapted and applied by anyone who sincerely wants to find meaning in modern circumstances and who wants to make the world a more humane place to live.

Allow me a little more autobiography. I am an instructor at Moraine Valley Community College, but I also have professional lay ministry credentials. I have been the campus ministry contact at the college for over twenty years. I also serve Sacred Heart Church as a part-time pastoral minister, and I serve on the boards of several Christian agencies and organizations.

Most of the people I meet during the week are sincere Christians, although I am also blessed with several Jewish and Muslim colleagues and friends. Most of these Christians, however, are largely unconcerned about internal church matters. The students and staff at my community college, my business associates, ordinary people in Sacred Heart parish, and people in my neighborhood are not oriented toward lay ministry—at least they don't use such language. They are focused on careers, on relationships, and on cultural or social issues.

To focus on one group, the Christian students at my college are not—with some exceptions—opposed to the church. They are not on a crusade to change internal church policies. At the same time, they are hard-pressed to articulate how their Christian faith pertains to their career choice, to their dealings with coworkers or neighbors, to societal issues, or even to all but the most general of family dilemmas.

Many of these students live a Christian life. The rate for Sunday worship among the Protestant students has declined only slightly in the past thirty years; among the Catholic students the rate has held constant since 1974. My students volunteer in their community and are concerned about personal ethics. They have some Christian habits of the heart. What they often lack, in my opinion, are Christian habits of the mind and of the imagination. They do not have a grand philosophy that might help them on the job, around the home, or in the community.

My students know they are supposed to do good and shun evil. They are not, however, taught how to translate their basic personal ethic into a sophisticated social analysis that sustains them through years of struggle for non-utopian reforms. My students are not yet acquainted with an ethic that allows for contradictions and compromise, one that critiques good policies that have gone bad, one that goes beyond freestanding codes and advances a holistic outlook premised on a society of virtuous citizens.

When reflecting about the students at my college, I often think about a challenging paragraph in the *Pastoral Constitution on the Church in the Modern World,* one of the key documents of Vatican II. After praising accomplishments in science, technology, commerce, and culture, the document asks: "What is the meaning and value of this feverish activity? How should all these things be used? To the achievement of what goal are the strivings of individuals and societies heading?"

These are perfect questions for my students, who are inundated with factoids, loaded with clichés, and busy with many obligations. Beneath it all, however, they are innocent of purpose. They are blessed with opportunity but deprived of ends. They are members of a prosperous society but are wandering in a teleological desert, to use a phrase from John Haughey, SJ, of Chicago. Yet when they are able or forced to turn off the distractions, they are awash in questions of purpose. My students and many other young adults are dealing with the other vocation crisis (the first crisis being the shortage of priests and religious); that is, a crisis of meaning.

Christian social thought is about ends, about the purpose of things. When presented correctly, the Christian worldview, with its emphasis on the common good, is a collective outlook on ultimate purposes. And so in my opinion, a presentation of Christian social principles is timely. This book is written for my students (whose average age is twenty-nine) and for other people of whatever age who seek some larger meaning in life.

This book is not primarily a call to action but an invitation to sift the myriad activities of life through a screen of Christian philosophy. By naming some Christian social principles and by examining three areas of life (work, the neighborhood, and the family), this book provides a way of thinking that gives the isolated episodes of life a deeper personal meaning and wider public purpose.

There are people who find meaning in their work and who contribute to society without drawing upon religious principles. There are also many people who, at least by one set of measures, practice religion but do not find meaning in their work and community life. My experience, however, corroborated by some research says that when people intelligently and comprehensively live their faith they are more likely to find their work meaningful and significant to others.

In the poem *Dry Salvages*, T. S. Eliot remarks that too often we "have the experience but miss the meaning." Equipped with a guiding philosophy or a set of principles, young adults will have a chance to be protagonists in the story they are writing. Combine these social principles with a disciplined prayer life and a practical spirituality (which includes liturgy, a support system, a routine of generosity, and skilled citizenship) and the result will be an army of confident and competent people, ready to help God complete the work of creation and redemption.

1

The Christian Vocation

> The laity, by their very vocation, seek the kingdom of God by engaging in temporal affairs and by ordering them to the plan of God. They live in the world, that is, in each and in all the secular professions and occupations....They can work for the sanctification of the world from within, in the manner of leaven.
>
> —*Dogmatic Constitution on the Church*

V. Paul Kenney, a physicist at a university in Tennessee, learned that four of his colleagues were Christian only when, while away at a conference, they all showed up for Mass at a church near the hotel. "By and large," observes Kenney, "scientists do not tell their colleagues that they are Christian, and they tend not to identify themselves as scientists to their pastors and fellow parishioners."

This split between faith and daily life applies as well to executives, civil servants, students, lawyers, social workers, and many more. The implication is not that Christians are terribly immoral on the job or around the community. It is, rather, that Christians are not very conscious that their workaday life is a primary expression of their response to God, that work itself puts holiness into life. From another angle, Christians do not normally pray and worship in a way that allows their work, family, and community life to shape and challenge that prayer. They do not, in an image suggested by William Byron, SJ, begin the Sunday offertory procession on the previous Monday.

This split between Sunday and Monday is curious because Vatican II, a watershed event in modern Christianity, signaled a major shift in the relationship between faith and the wider world of work, politics, art, education, and civic life. Unlike a sect that tries to maintain a safe distance (and thus its purity) from the established centers of culture, commerce, and industry, Vatican II envisioned a community of Christians at the center of human enterprise.

The *sine qua non* of the Vatican II understanding of church-in-the-world is a refurbished notion of the laity. In fact, Vatican II collapses without a lay model. According to Vatican II, Christians live their faith by sustaining and improving familial, cultural, economic, political, and social institutions. The Christian vocation is lived by attending office meetings, by participating in a local union, by agitating for improved delivery of services at the college, hospital, or agency, and by hundreds of other daily activities. As insiders to society, Christians are called to be salt and light in their professions, occupations, and states in life.

Obviously the Vatican II model must be very broad and generic. Concrete circumstances vary in different societies, different historical exigencies, and even in different neighborhoods. Nevertheless, a lay-centered model serves as a benchmark against which to measure Christian life today. The vision of Vatican II is so refreshing, yet the surface has hardly been scratched on its key theme—that the church is the people of God involved in service to the modern world.

Why hasn't the vision of Vatican II concerning a lay-centered church caught on more widely among North Americans? This is a perplexing issue, because the ideas Vatican II put forth on liturgy, ecumenism, Scripture, and religious life were, for the most part, received with enthusiasm and have been implemented—although more remains to be done. The lack of appreciation for a lay-centered church is doubly ironic because Catholics, in a statistical population that includes the new immigrants, are now the wealthiest and best-educated gentile group in the United States. If the connection between faith and daily life were fully appropriated, Catholics would have enormous influence.

There are several theories as to why there is a lack of understanding of the lay vocation. Some people argue that the success of Christians is itself a cause of the problem. Many Christian politicians, engineers, administrators, executives, and other professionals do not want to hear that baptism calls them to be salt and light in the world, for that might jeopardize their positions.

North American individualism is the culprit, according to a similar argument. Religion on this continent is, in an oft-repeated phrase, "a private matter." It might be all right, in the style of evangelicals, to read the Bible on the train or meet for prayer during lunch hour, but it is almost un-American to introduce a reform in business policy based on publicly stated principles of faith. (Even reading the Bible on the train is viewed suspiciously by the wider culture.)

The Chicago Declaration of Christian Concern

There is another, very controversial explanation for why Christians have yet to practice the Vatican II teaching on the Christian vocation. In Advent of 1977, a group of forty-three prominent Catholics issued the Chicago Declaration of Christian Concern (see Appendix for full text), which argued that, unintentionally, all of the attention given to lay ministry inside the church in the years after Vatican II left people with the impression that they best express their faith by serving as a lector, eucharistic minister, catechist, and the like. As the Chicago Declaration states:

> Although the teaching of Vatican II on the ministry of the laity [in the world] is forceful and represents one of the Council's most notable achievements, in recent years it seems to have all but vanished from the consciousness and agendas of many sectors within the church. It is our experience that a wholesome and significant movement within the church—the involvement of lay people in many church ministries—has led to a devaluation of the unique ministry of lay women and men [to the world]. The tendency has been to see lay ministry as involvement in some church related activity, e.g. religious education, pastoral care for the sick or elderly, or readers in church on Sunday.

The Declaration concludes that a preoccupation with internal lay ministry can unwittingly "distract the laity from the apostolic potential that lies at the core of their professional and occupational lives."

How, in practice, might attention to internal lay ministry slight the lay vocation to the world? Here is an example. The liturgy team at a Chicago parish decided to make some minor changes in the Holy Thursday liturgy. After the priests had gathered around the altar to renew their vows, women religious were called forth from the congregation to do the same. Next, all the lay ministers of the parish were invited to stand in front of the congregation and renew their pledge of service to the people. This action had the benefit of taking the spotlight off the clergy and drawing attention to forty or fifty parish volunteers. Neglected in the planning for this recognition, however, were all those in the pews who act as "ministers" by driving an ambulance, building homes, teaching college students, parenting teenagers, or caring for an infirm relative.

To mention a second example, a pastor in California recently notified his flock that "every baptized Catholic who regularly receives communion has an obligation to serve for a time as a minister during Mass." Where did the pastor find a citation for this obligation? When did the pastor last use his bulletin to remind his flock of their baptismal obligation to vote or to read the newspaper or to oppose racism?

Gregory Pierce, a businessman from Chicago, supplies a third example from a parish bulletin that applauds sixty-one former "pew potatoes" who joined the ranks of the parish's official lay ministers:

> Equating those who do not participate in a lay ministry with couch potatoes who sit in front of a TV might be cute. I too am guilty of calling other people names to make a point. For example, I refer to those who spend an inordinate amount of time in parish-related activities as churchaholics. However, people forgo involvement in parish ministries for many reasons. Some of the pew potatoes might very well be caring for a sick relative or working an extra job. These people are no less active parishioners in the sense of living the gospel.
>
> One of the many ministries that people in the parish in question could sign up for is (I swear) Adult Volleyball. Perhaps we can arrange a game between the pew potatoes and the churchaholics—winner take all.

These are small examples, perhaps, but ones, according to signers of the Chicago Declaration, indicative of a careless mindset.

Ministry Inside or Outside?

The Chicago Declaration has been debated in classrooms, magazines, journals, and at conferences for several years. It has gained many supporters and some persistent critics. In particular, the Chicago Declaration is criticized for denigrating the marvelous contributions of lay ministers. Don't blame generous volunteers and other dedicated lay ministers for a problem they did not cause, the criticism goes. Lay ministers should be affirmed while still challenged to assist the entire church in its effort to turn outward.

The Chicago Declaration, and the analysis it represents, is also criticized for reintroducing an unnecessary distinction between the role of the clergy and the role of the laity—a distinction which, by the way, is found in the documents of Vatican II. The key word in ministry today, this criticism says, is collaboration. Priests and religious have every right, indeed a duty, to join the struggle for peace and justice by engaging in temporal affairs. By the same token, lay people have a right to participate in the liturgy as lectors and eucharistic ministers, and in parish life as parish council members, catechists, and more.

Over the years supporters of the Chicago Declaration have repeatedly explained that their analysis is not meant as a personal criticism of any priest, religious, permanent deacon, professional lay minister or parish volunteer. Nor is the analysis intended to be against lay ministry as such. In fact, the Chicago Declaration itself says that the lay ministry movement is "wholesome and significant." The unintended problem, the Chicago Declaration supporters persist, is that somehow, amid the post-Vatican II movements toward lay ministry and parish renewal, the ordinary Christian has been left with the impression that fuller church involvement means internal ministry. Thus the Chicago Declaration supporters were not surprised when a major study of Catholicism in North America defined "core Catholics" as those who devote extra time to liturgical functions or parish activities.

As for the charge that the Chicago Declaration advances a false dichotomy between church employees and laity, its supporters tell the story of a priest who spoke to a chapter of the lay organization Serra International. In his own opinion this priest, assigned to a high school, brings "something extra to the classroom," something which "an ordinary mathematics teacher cannot bring." The Chicago Declaration supporters use this story to acknowledge that there are circumstances where an ordained priest or church employee rightly takes on the details of teaching mathematics, maintaining a building, administering a hospital, or participating in civic life. But, the Chicago Declaration supporters insist, that priest or church employee performs those functions simply because he or she is a competent leader—nothing more or less.

By the same token, there are many circumstances where a non-ordained person or a non-church employee should proclaim the gospel, prepare others for sacraments, even preach. Supporters of the Chicago Declaration take umbrage, however, at reports like the series in an Arizona Catholic newspaper that predicate lay ministry on the declining number of priests. "We're calling on lay people to fill the need of the priest shortage," the newspaper quoted a parish's pastoral care coordinator. "If we had a lot of priests, I don't think this [visiting of the sick] would have happened." Christians do not visit the sick simply because of a parish program but because of their fidelity to the corporal works of mercy, the Chicago Declaration supporters would remind the coordinator.

Likewise, the locus for preaching the gospel, preparing others for sacraments or preaching—much less for doing the works of mercy and justice—is not restricted to the sanctuary or to an official church program. The people of God, say the Chicago Declaration supporters, proclaim the gospel throughout the week because of the responsibility given at baptism, not because they are para-clerics.

John Maine of St. Catherine of Siena parish in Miami, Florida, has introduced a "work dedication" into the liturgy. On six Sundays a year workers in a specific occupation are blessed and asked to commit themselves to Christian values on the job. The blessing has been given to healthcare workers, business people, teachers, homemakers, construction workers, civil servants, police, and others. Maine came up with the idea because "the church's attention to the role of the laity has been overwhelmingly toward lay ministry inside the church, as opposed to the laity's primary role in their work and community." The parish and the diocese sponsor sessions for lectors and other lay ministers, he says, but short-order cooks don't have any programs to reflect on work and gospel values. The upshot, says Maine, is that when asked about their primary religious role, Christians do not think about work.

Defining Vocation

The Chicago Declaration's analysis also has implications for how the church currently understands the relative shortage of candidates for ordained priesthood and religious life. With only a handful of exceptions, diocesan newspapers, diocesan vocation offices, those in religious orders, campus ministers, and other church leaders use the phrase "vocation crisis" synonymously with the relative shortage of ordained priests and vowed religious. This vocation crisis, as defined by church leaders, is the number one factor (money running a close second) driving all practical decisions about the mission of the church. Contrary to the message of Vatican II, the unacknowledged assumption is that there are no vocations other than those to the priesthood and religious life. Crises (both of numbers and of meaning) in the vocations to business, sociology, nursing, journalism, or homemaking are irrelevant to the mission of the church, it is assumed.

In diocesan newspapers, feature stories about vocations are usually about seminarians, priests, religious, and permanent deacons. Decisions about opening or closing Catholic parishes or schools always account for trends in religious vocations but rarely for trends in other vocations. Posters and literature from diocesan vocation offices always picture seminarians or novices, never carpenters, husbands and wives, architects, or scientists.

Dorothy Sayers, best known for her whodunits, was convinced that the real vocation crisis was the church's failure to recognize the sacredness of everyday work. Unfortunately, "the church's approach to an intelligent carpenter is usually confined to exhorting him [or her] not to be drunk and disorderly in leisure hours, and to come to church on Sundays." What the church should be telling the carpenter, Sayers continues, is that the very first demand your vocation makes upon you is to "make good tables." Yet "the official church wastes time and energy, and moreover commits a sacrilege, in demanding that workers should neglect their proper vocation in order to do [internal lay ministry]." Worse yet, when it comes to music for worship or the skill of running a parish meeting, "the church will tolerate or permit a pious intention to excuse work so ugly, so pretentious, so tawdry and twaddling, so insincere and insipid, so bad as to shock and horrify any decent worker."

Ironically, the narrow definition of the vocation crisis may actually be contributing to the relative shortage of ordained priests and vowed religious. According to the late Cardinal Joseph Bernardin, the "way of stating the problem may itself be part of the problem." The best method for increasing the number of priests and religious, Bernardin suggested, was to foster a vocation culture in which all young adult Christians understand their careers and their states in life as a response to the universal call to holiness. The assumption that priesthood and religious life "are the only real vocations," Bernardin argued, "can only worsen the crisis posed by the shortage of priests and religious."

Anglican Archbishop George Carey of Canterbury paints a picture of a church that understands the Christian vocation in its proper, universal sense:

I want to challenge a theology and a history which automatically assumes...that what we do as Christians in the church is more significant than what we do in our daily work as executives, university professors, engineers, lawyers and so on....We need to see at the center of God's mission not the splendid work of the church, but the equally splendid wilderness of the world—where there are few places for Christians to hide, where moral and ethical signposts are blurred or nonexistent, and where we are [sometimes] outnumbered by the indifferent, the unholy, and the culture despisers of our day.

I am proposing...a suspension of all normal church activities to enable a start from a wholly new perspective. That is, not to seek survival as an institution but to aim to be the church of Jesus

Christ in the world....The TV producer will consider how, exactly, she or he brings Christianity into the presentation of programs; the engineer will reflect on his or her design, professional relationships and influence on others from a Christian standpoint; the corporate director will view the policy proposals of management within a perspective of servant-leadership....

The natural consequence of turning the church inside out [will be to question] how far does this corporation, this college, this town council serve the kingdom of God, both in policy objectives and operational procedures.

2

The Journey Outward

The split between the faith which many profess and their daily lives deserves to be counted among the most serious errors of our age.

—Pastoral Constitution on the Church in the Modern World

The Second Vatican Council concluded in December of 1965 with, fittingly, the promulgation of two outward looking documents, the *Declaration on Religious Freedom* and the *Pastoral Constitution on the Church in the Modern World*. Each calls for the church, as the people of God, to engage the world "that God so loves."

Comments Robert McAfee Brown, a Protestant observer at the Council: "It would have been possible for the Second Vatican Council to concern itself solely with internal affairs—the reform of the liturgy, a fresh look at seminary education and so on. It is highly significant," however, that from beginning to end Vatican II "turned outward to examine the ways in which a church, subject to reform and renewal, should relate to those beyond its walls."

Had Vatican II "decided to concentrate exclusively on the internal reform of the church and to say nothing at all about the church's relations to the modern world," it would have been "a partial success," admits Msgr. George Higgins, another observer at the Council. To the credit of the Holy Spirit, however, Vatican II took "advantage of a long-awaited opportunity to engage [humankind] in fraternal conversation." The entire tone of Vatican II, especially as found in the document

Pastoral Constitution on the Church in the Modern World, is "to enter into a dialogue with the modern world," Higgins concludes.

The leaders of Vatican II can today rightly be described as outward-looking Christians. In the Vatican II vision of the church, women and men—personally and directly—bring justice, compassion, and reconciliation to the world, as those women and men interact with their families, their neighbors, their coworkers, and the poor in their backyards and around the world. In painting such a vision, Vatican II produced the outline for a worldly spirituality—something not often lifted up in the Christian tradition. Because it takes the incarnation seriously, it is a spirituality that propels Christians into the world of work, family, and neighborhood.

It must be admitted, however, that the Vatican II vision is at the moment a buried treasure. It desperately awaits confident and competent Christians who are eager to take the initiative on the job, around the home, and in the neighborhood.

Preliminary Obstacles

Unfortunately, even before such Christians carry the spark of Vatican II into the rough and tumble worlds of family, neighborhood, and job, they must overcome some obstacles. One of those, the preoccupation by some Christians with internal church matters, has been previously discussed and will only be mentioned here.

There are still sermons, parish meetings, pieces of literature, designs and plans in church agencies, and foggy notions in the minds of people that limit the definition of church. An assumption still lingers that a committed Christian is one who knows the technical details of diocesan and parish structure, one who speaks a churchy language and, optimally, one who volunteers for or is employed by a church organization. There are too few forums in which workaday Christians are encouraged to see their cities and towns as places in need of healing, too few sermons that encourage them to be partisans of justice, and not enough support groups that challenge them as spouses, citizens, and workers.

This limiting assumption encourages a journey inward rather than the Vatican II vision of a journey outward. Please note: it is not only conservatives who are walking the inward path. Recently a coalition of reform organizations bought a full-page ad in a major newspaper to announce that because of imperfections in the institutional church many Christians "are crippled" from addressing "pressing issues in the home, the workplace, and the political process."

Bernard Häring, CSSR, who is no stranger to criticism from church authorities, has a different attitude:

> I can understand why people who concentrate their attention solely on [internal church] institutions become disillusioned. But our faith forbids us to take such a narrow view. For me the church is embodied and made real in the many exemplary Christian families I have known....I have experienced the church through encounters with humble, insightful saints today.

Of course the church needs internal reform. More people need to be recruited to the priesthood, religious life, and professional lay ministry. Systematic approaches to fundraising for parishes, schools, and other church institutions need to be implemented and maintained. Church policies on marriage and divorce need to be administered in as pastoral a way as possible. The ordained priesthood either has to include qualified women or a clear, non-fundamentalist reason for gender exclusion needs to be articulated.

Each Christian has to devote some time, energy, or money to the internal reform of the institutional church. A few Christians well serve the entire community by making a career out of internal reform. But a disservice is done to the Christian community when it is implied that attention to the internal matters of the church makes one a more involved Christian than someone who is uninterested in the comings and goings of chancery personnel, programs, and policies. In no case should a Christian ever feel so "crippled" by a cautious prelate or a restricting church policy that she or he refrains from shouldering her or his baptismal burden, from taking the initiative in the home, the workplace, or in political life.

An Activist Spirituality

Gregory Pierce—husband, father of three, businessman, denizen of

city streets, and diehard Chicago Cubs fan—is "looking for a spirituality of noise, crowds and activism." He is tired of sermons that advise
him to "get away from the world and discover God." Pierce, who
describes himself as "piety impaired," wants "a spirituality that will
help me find the meaningful, the eternal, the transcendent, the divine
in the midst of the hustle and bustle of daily life."

Pierce is dealing with the second preliminary obstacle to developing a Vatican II spirituality: Most centers of spirituality, retreat houses,
spiritual books, courses on Christian renewal, religious programs on
television, and even many parish-based spiritual events specialize in
the journey inward. One could quickly get the impression that holiness
is nearly the same thing as getting in touch with your feelings. In fact,
in many Christian circles spirituality is equated with the Myers-Briggs
typologies, or centering prayer, or the enneagram, or walking a
labyrinth.

Correctly understood, writes Thomas Merton, "the spiritual life is not
a life of quiet withdrawal, a hothouse growth of artificial ascetic practices....It is in the ordinary duties and labors of life that the Christian
can and should develop spiritual union with God." Such an understanding, explains Merton, has implications for work, which "is by
itself capable of contributing much to the spiritual life." The place of
work in the spiritual life is not, Merton insists, a matter of "interior, sub-
jective adjustment." Serving on workplace committees, for example, is
itself part of Christian holiness. "The individual Christian will do more
to sanctify his [or her] work by becoming intelligently concerned with
social order and with effective political means to improve social conditions, than he [or she] will ever be able to do merely by interior and
personal spiritual efforts."

Until he died in November of 1992, my family was blessed by the
friendship of Fr. Dennis Geaney, a person who had a Vatican II vision
both before and after the Council. After suffering a heart attack,
Geaney developed the habit of taking long walks in the neighborhood.
Along the way he would stop in small factories, auto repair shops,
social agencies, and people's homes. What he gleaned from those
walks helped Geaney articulate a spirituality for the laity in his sermons, in his books, and in a weekly bulletin column titled

"Confessions of a Streetwalker." A genuine spirituality for the laity, says Geaney, would

> seem at first to be the opposite of what the classical spiritual writers call the conversion to God. Our times call for a conversion to the world. Too many people like to shy away from the world when they become reconverted to God. Too often they want to love God away from the stock exchange, courts of justice, factories, offices, or marts of trade.

Many of the dominant themes in Christian spirituality derive from a monastic tradition. To be fair, work has a place in that tradition. But for the monks work is a backdrop to contemplation, a tool for prayer. This leads to a spirituality in which good intentions are more important than competent action. There are "disastrous consequences," Geaney warns, if lay spirituality is simply something borrowed from the monastery. For the laity, work in and of itself must count. Work is not to be merely tolerated; it is a call

> to complete the work of creation and to cooperate in the work of redemption....Work itself must become a way to God, not merely an interlude between morning and evening prayers. In fact, prayer cannot be defined as time snatched from the messy world....Every bed made, potato peeled, or ton of steel poured is the incense of praise rising above the suburban chimney and the black clouds of the steel mill.

For a full-time Christian, a spirituality that is practiced in a state of activity is preferable to, if not superior to, any spirituality that is practiced in a state of withdrawal. An incense-filled chapel is no more holy than a smoke-filled caucus room. (This image, of course, overlooks the fact that cigarettes are unwholesome, unholy.) A sin-scarred world is, for the full-time Christian, as much a place for holiness as any sanctuary.

Beyond Individual Piety

Kathleen Norris, a popular poet and writer, was invited to be a guest homilist at a certain parish. The pastor told her to focus on personal spirituality. But as Norris prepared the sermon she realized "that the whole notion of a personal spirituality [is] an impossibility, a contradiction in terms." When the word "personal" is used in a religious context, the meaning is usually private. "But Christianity, like its ancestor Judaism, is inescapably communal," says Norris. "I've...become increasingly wary of what strikes me as a growing tendency to treat the soul as just one more [individual] consumer on the American landscape and spirituality as the commodity that fulfills every whim."

This focus on the personal comes to North American Christians by way of Protestantism, especially its Calvinist influences. People on this continent are aware that Christianity has a social mission. In fact, North American Christians are exemplary in their willingness to build and support church-sponsored schools, hospitals, and agencies. As individuals and as congregations, North American Christians send donations to every corner of the globe. Yet, when it comes to prayer and the spiritual life, North American Christians consider their faith to be "a personal matter between God and me."

Pop psychology and the New Age movement support this individualistic pietism by implying that wisdom is nothing more than the fulfillment of personal potential with little attention to broader social concerns. Many North Americans, as they move away from immigrant enclaves, adopt an individualistic approach to spirituality. In fact, Eugene McCarraher of the University of Delaware is only half-joking when he says that the grandchildren of immigrants now practice "Starbucks Catholicism." They are imbued with "a therapeutic spirituality" whose "spiritual preceptors" are "the self-help, inspirational crowd of Marianne Williamson, Deepak Chopra, M. Scott Peck, Paul Wilkes, and Thomas Moore—all very popular with Catholic readers."

In these years after Vatican II, however, a smaller number of Christians have caught a glimpse of another kind of spirituality—one in which they, in the company of others, encounter God in the give and take of marriage, family life, business, civic endeavors, and worldly affairs. The United States Catholic bishops refer to this new type of spirituality in their pastoral letter, *Economic Justice for All*:

Holiness is not limited to the sanctuary or to moments of private prayer; it is a call to direct our whole heart and life toward God and according to God's plan for the world. For the laity holiness is achieved in the midst of the world, in family, in community, in friendships, in work, in leisure, in citizenship....

We need a spirituality that calls forth and supports lay initiative and witness not just in our churches but also in business, in the labor movement, in the professions, in education, and in public life. Our faith is not just a weekend obligation, a mystery to be celebrated around the altar on Sunday. It is a pervasive reality to be practiced everyday in homes, offices, factories, schools, and businesses across our land.

The same idea was in the mind of Fr. Isaac Hecker, founder of the Paulists, as he tried in the nineteenth century to replace pastoral practices inherited from Europe and the monasteries with ones more suited to the North American ethos:

Our age is not an age of martyrdom, nor an age of hermits, nor a monastic age. Although it has its martyrs, its recluses, and its monastic communities, these are not, and are not likely to be, its prevailing types of Christian perfection. Our age lives in its busy marts, in counting rooms, in shops, in homes and in the varied relations that form human society and it is into these that sanctity is to be introduced.

A Spirituality for the Journey Outward

A new type of spirituality, designed for busy Christians on the job, in the family, and around the neighborhood, is being called a spirituality of work. To be correctly understood, the spirituality of work, for better or worse, has to distinguish itself from other ideas:

The spirituality of work has to depart from all spiritual traditions, including those influenced by Aristotle and other ancient Greek philosophers, that express a preference for leisure or contemplation and sometimes even contempt for work. At the other extreme, the spirituality of work does not endorse the view contained in some strands of the Protestant ethic that successful work in itself is a sign of God's election.

The spirituality of work must also heave aside any notion that work is the result of original sin. A correct reading of Genesis shows that even before the fall people had to work. Their job was "to till and keep the garden of Eden," or in a poetic translation, "to dress paradise." Work therefore is not the result of original sin; it is not a punishment for disobedience.

After dispelling incorrect notions, the spirituality of work can develop several positive themes:

To be called a worker is to have a title of dignity. The spirituality of work has no patience for those in a skyscraper office who snobbishly eschew the label "worker" in favor of "professional" or "executive" or other subcategories. The spirituality of work likewise finds no contradiction in pairing the words "unemployed worker." Nor, unlike some women's magazines, does the spirituality of work exclude homemakers (or volunteers or students) from the title "worker." What gives work its dignity, says the spirituality of work, is not the type of work being done but the fact that the worker is a human being who is participating in God's ongoing creative and salvific activity.

The world of work, according to this new type of spirituality, is more than an individual affair. In refreshing contrast to the highly individualistic nature of work in North America (despite the rhetoric of collaboration and teamwork), the spirituality of work insists that work creates bonds of solidarity among coworkers, and between workers and others in the community. The primary intention in God's original job description for his workers was the unification of humanity. Therefore, the spirituality of work points toward an economy in which each person sees himself or herself laboring at the one great workbench, of which he or she is a part-owner.

According to the spirituality of work, a job can never be regarded as simply a necessary means to achieving private ends. People work not just to get money to buy more things. The real virtue of work is to allow people to become fully human. Pope John Paul II tries to express this notion with his easily misunderstood principle of the priority of labor over capital. He is not taking sides in a union-management dispute. He is, rather, asserting that each worker should participate in the economy and share in responsibility and creativity at the workbench. Furthermore, the work of each person and of each company must contribute not only to the owners but also to the whole society. The spirituality of work thus challenges a business culture that would scoff at the notion of stakeholders.

The spirituality of work is also critical of a culture in which careerism is substituted for calling. It should be a somewhat normal occurrence, says the spirituality of work, for a person's deepest gladness to meet the world's deepest hunger. That is, workers should be able to live their vocations on the job, around the home, and in the neighborhood. The spirituality of work advocates for an economy and a culture in which work contributes to the total growth of workers, not merely to their paychecks or portfolios.

Spirituality, a sage once said, is awareness. Ah, but awareness of what? Awareness of the butterfly in the caterpillar, of the sunflower in the seed? The spirituality of work encourages people to be aware of the grace in the house that contains smelly sneakers and dirty laundry; grace in the office that contains too many piles of file folders; grace in the classroom that contains noisy students and a malfunctioning loud-speaker. The spirituality of work encourages people to look for God and respond to God amid daily chores, among family members, and in the community.

Edward Schillebeeckx, OP, the Belgian theologian, tells this story. During his first night in the Dominican seminary Schillebeeckx got up at three o'clock in the morning to listen to the chanting of the Liturgy of the Hours. In a letter to his father he described this as the most exhilarating experience of his young life. His father wrote him back: "That same night your baby brother was crying. Your mother and I were up all night trying to quiet him."

There is a spirituality that is suited to Dominicans who chant the Liturgy of the Hours at three o'clock in the morning. There is another spirituality, however, more suited to parents who try to quiet a baby at three o'clock in the morning. The spirituality of work, which is only now being developed, is for Jesus' friend Martha and all others who are busy with so many things. It is a style of awareness that presumes something divine is below the mundane surface, and helps ordinary people to work, study, and play in a more expansive way.

3

A Spirituality of Work

The whole church has "a particular duty to form a spirituality of work which will help all people come closer, through work, to God the Creator and Redeemer."

—Laborem Exercens

There is no simple blueprint for a spirituality of work. It does not yet have one abiding definition, one mandatory handbook, or one compulsory set of disciplines. People work in many different settings and are engaged in a variety of family and community activities. Something that makes sense today may not fit tomorrow, as new relationships are formed and different commitments made in our lives. A spirituality of work, however, can give some touchstones, some disciplines, a framework, perhaps, for a style of holiness that puts Christians in better touch with God precisely as they touch the world around them.

This spirituality is for active people, but it requires regular reflection on the meaning of work on the job, around the home, and in the neighborhood. It is not, as in more individualistic spiritualities, restricted to so-called sacred times and places. The spirituality of work alerts people to God already present in the world—especially around the office and in the plant, on campus and at the restaurant, in the midst of phone calls and e-mail messages. It is a spirituality that encourages people to look for God and respond to God amid appointments and decisions, at family gatherings and during contentious community meetings.

The Search for Meaning in the Marketplace

Why are managers, business theorists, service providers, sales representatives, professionals, and many other workers asking questions about the meaning of work? There are several reasons:

• The scope of the national and international economy has changed the perspective from which workers relate their individual contributions to wider purposes. It is not easy to have a sense of connection from an isolated division within a large multinational firm, delivering one specialized service or product.

• The anxiety about who really wins in a booming economy also raises questions about what workers do and why they do it. What does it mean when more than one-third of the top industrial companies disappear or completely alter their product every ten years? What does it mean that the wage gap and wealth gap between the top five percent and the remaining ninety-five percent of workers is steadily widening? What does it mean that thirty percent of companies employing more than 500 people and fifty-five percent of those employing fewer than thirty fail within five years? Is there any such thing as a career anymore?

• A new style of management challenges past practices but also raises new questions. Millions of dollars and thousands of hours are spent each month addressing the topic of employee morale, company by company, department by department. New social science theory, new communication technology, new definitions of customer, supplier, employee, and stakeholder have all contributed to the search for meaning in the workplace.

• Wholesale changes occurring in family life greatly affect the workplace and people's expectations there. The proportional increase of women and mothers in the paid labor force, one of the most significant social changes since World War II, raises many concerns and issues in business.

• The consumer and corporate responsibility movements also add new questions as they heighten expectations about integrity in the workplace.

• There has been renewed interest in work theory. Management books and journals, once confined to university libraries but now plentiful on bookstore shelves and even in supermarkets, are all addressing topics that concern the meaning of work. Books describing management techniques that communicate corporate purpose and values to workers become bestsellers. There are hundreds of books about so-called "excellent companies," those in which women and men are encouraged to take stock of themselves, to discuss what they want out of life, to articulate their beliefs, and to state how their jobs contribute to the rest of their lives. Words like service, values, and fulfillment—words that only a few years ago were never heard at work—are now routinely found in mission statements that are hammered out during employee retreats.

It is, again, more than a coincidence that the marketplace is reassessing the meaning of work at the same time some segments in Christianity are advocating an outward-directed spirituality. Both the marketplace and Christianity are, as John Paul II explains, beginning to recognize that work is a fundamental dimension of human existence, and that work is a key to the values of the human enterprise.

Spirituality of Work vs. the Spirituality-in-Business Movement

The spirituality of work has something in common with the mushrooming spirituality-in-business movement. Both put the spiritual life in the context of daily responsibilities. The two have some different assumptions, however. A contrast between them further explicates the spirituality of work.

Within the spirituality-in-business movement there is an eclectic mix of management techniques, New Age seminars, serious study of the Bible and the Qur'an during lunch hour, "soul committees" at several major companies, chaplains serving in the personnel department, and thousands of executive meetings on topics such as "core values" and "serving the whole person." This movement has been featured in *Business Week*, the *Christian Science Monitor*, the *Los Angeles Times*, the *New York Times*, and other publications. The Spirit of Health Institute in Richmond, California, one of the movement's hubs, has published a spirituality-in-business directory that lists hundreds of books, consultants, training programs, videos, annual conferences, and much more.

The spirituality-in-business movement first tilts out of sync with the spirituality of work when it includes themes from the gospel of wealth and success, an unfortunate byproduct of the Protestant Reformation. By contrast, the tradition that shapes a spirituality of work finds no parallel between God's favor and financial success, per se. In fact, just the opposite is true: the spirituality of work tends to emphasize God's special concern for the unfortunate.

When it comes to judging the moral character of the marketplace, the spirituality-in-business movement is also at odds with a spirituality of work. One underlying theme found in the spirituality-in-business movement is the depravity of business culture and the need to bring Christ into the marketplace. The spirituality of work is, of course, alert to the world's flaws but is also optimistic about the grace that abounds in the office, the factory, the shop, the home, and the neighborhood. The spirituality of work is thus not an attempt to spiritualize work or even to carry God into the marketplace. More properly, the spirituality of work helps Christians cooperate with God, who is already lurking about, often masquerading as a supplier, a customer, an employee, an elderly relative, or a student and whose glory is embedded, though imperfectly, in office routines, policy guidelines, legislation, art, and architecture.

To the spirituality-in-business movement, this saying of St. Thérèse of Lisieux is baffling: "Prayer arises, if at all, from incompetence, otherwise there is no need of prayer." In a spirituality of work, the saying packs some wisdom.

The spirituality-in-business movement and some other spiritual traditions are at times willing to overlook shoddiness because a given worker is a sincere Christian. The spirituality of work, by contrast, builds all the other virtues and disciplines on a bedrock of competence. Explains Charles DiSalvo of West Virginia University:

> Christians are called on to perfect the world. Therefore their work had better be good. If your work entails production, then it means building the best objects possible. If your work is service, then those services must be brought to the best possible completion.

This good work, DiSalvo explains, is normally done in the language and culture of a particular clinic, office, shop, or dock. There is no need to additionally spiritualize good work by wearing your religion on your sleeve. A person who follows a spirituality of work does not suddenly work in a new Christian way. In fact, it is unlikely that during a hectic day someone practicing a spirituality of work will ever consciously say: "I am a Christian business person or teacher who is trying to live a spirituality of work." Instead, such people will, hour by hour, try to work in a way that permits them to fully realize their whole self and in a way that allows others to be fully human.

The spirituality of work encompasses a person's response to the task at hand—a response that is professional, compassionate, skilled, and directed toward the common good. The spirituality of work, if it means anything at all, means doing good work. Professional competence, the key ingredient to successful endeavors, is not divorced in any way from the spirituality of work. Of course, competence must be surrounded by virtue: patience, humility, justice, longanimity, and others. But to those who presume that good intentions have merit, the spirituality of work shouts: only work done with competence and virtue is spiritual work.

The elegant prose directed to engineers by Samuel Florman applies to all those who are interested in a spirituality of work:

> Our work contributes to the well-being of our fellow humans. There are religious implications in technology—a little bit of cathedral in everything we build....[But] engineers are not missionaries. As professionals we pledge ourselves to public service, but I think this is stating the case backward. By being hardworking, responsible, dependable and creative we end up being of service to the community, as well as enhancing our own pride and pleasure. A kindly, generous, well-intentioned, even saintly engineer may still be an inept engineer, that is, a bad engineer whose work does not serve the public well....In technical work competence is more good than goodness.

Mixing the Spiritual with Other Motives

The spirituality of work is down-to-earth and is compatible with concern for one's well-being. As Vatican II suggests, the purpose of work unfolds in various ways:

For while providing the substance of life for themselves and their families, women and men are performing their activities in such a way that appropriately benefits society. They can justly consider that by their labor they are unfolding the Creator's work, consulting the advantages of their brothers and sisters, and contributing by their personal industry to the realization in history of the divine plan. (*Constitution on the Church in the Modern World,* #34)

This statement from Vatican II reflects common experience. People rarely have a singular motive; instead, we commonly have different motives simultaneously. For example, a job provides a way of making a living; at the same time it is of service to humankind and contributes to God's plan of continuing creation. A spirituality of work is sophisticated enough to balance several motives—even those that seemingly compete with one another.

With a tolerance for mixed motives, a person practicing a spirituality of work will experience meaningful moments precisely as she or he plows through hundreds of unexciting tasks each week. A spirituality of work does not offer a detour from lease arrangements, plant maintenance, quarterly reports, or the Friday paycheck. It does not explicitly look heavenward nor does it consider work to be spiritual only to the extent it allows managers or employees to spend some company time and money on charitable activities. The spirituality of work is convinced that it is possible to work for ourselves and our families while at the same time benefiting the community and also contributing to God's plan.

The spirituality of work is also different from more individualistic spiritualities in its regard for institutions. A person practicing the spirituality of work, in other words, takes into account the context of work—the norms and customs of a firm, a department, an industry, and even the larger economic system. Acknowledged or not, these business norms and customs are of a moral character and over time, apart from the intentions of any one worker, they condition people for the good or for the bad.

The spirituality of work appreciates that some companies and some economic systems, because they are well-organized and consonant with the best of human aspirations, make it easier for people to be holy. On the other hand, when companies and other institutions are poorly organized or out of touch with what is good, they hurt the people they are intended to serve and, therefore, actually can impede the spiritual life.

Christians who practice a spirituality of work must be stewards of God's creation as it unfolds in all the places where people work—in neighborhoods, medical departments, sales offices, professional associations, unions, and other institutions. Unfortunately, "stewardship" has become a code word to signal that an appeal for money is on the way. Yet, according to William Byron, SJ, the word has a much wider meaning. Stewardship, he says, is the obligation to monitor and improve the social system. It is "closely linked with the notion of economic justice and is not, for example, unrelated to worldwide ecological and environmental concerns. If we waste or abuse resources, we are violating a trust."

As stewards of society, says Charles DiSalvo,

> Christians have a responsibility to direct the institutions we have formed toward the common good. This will involve awareness of the rich heritage of social teaching; allowing that teaching to inform actions at work and in the community; and even weighing career choices and civic involvements against those teachings.

The spirituality of work requires its practitioners to join with like-minded people (of whatever religious tradition) in the company, a union, or a professional or civic association, to improve production, service, labor, and social policies. In contrast to programs where the goal is to soothe workers' psyches, the spirituality of work, by including this notion of stewardship, can raise the anxiety level for a period of time.

The Work of the People

In another contrast with individualistic spiritualities, a spirituality of work is intimately linked with the liturgy, especially the Eucharist. This may sound odd when you first hear it. After all, isn't the Mass a special time for each person to be alone with God? Isn't liturgy the exact opposite of work? Not if liturgy is properly understood. The English word "liturgy" comes from the Greek *leitourgia*, which in the fifth century BC was a fusion of two terms standing for "people" and "work" to designate public tasks performed by citizens. Thus *leitourgia*, or liturgy, can be translated, "the work of the people in the public square," or simply, "people's work."

It is a corruption of the liturgy to think of it in individualistic terms. While Christians are always welcome to meditate and say personal prayers in church, the hour—more or less—of Sunday worship is a public, communal event. People worship together as family members, neighbors, workers, and, quite properly, in the company of strangers. The liturgy is designed precisely to send worshippers back to the world of work with enough collective spiritual energy to humanize the office, the store, the campus, the neighborhood, and the household.

Granted, people do not easily think about work as part of the eucharistic mystery or about the Eucharist as one of the tools needed for their work. Yet what is it that becomes God on the altar? Listen carefully to the Prayer Over the Gifts:

> Through your goodness we have this bread to offer, which earth has given and human hands have made....Through your goodness we have this wine to offer, fruit of the vine and work of human hands.

The body and blood of Jesus Christ are not in the form of wheat and grapes. It takes the work of human hands to fashion the gifts of God's creation into a form that will be consecrated.

The bread that is consecrated, broken, and shared at Mass represents all of the food that sustains humankind. It also represents the bread of science and technology, commerce, the arts, social service, even civilization itself. The wine that is poured and shared at Mass represents all of the fruit and vegetables harvested by migrant farm workers, transported by teamsters, stocked and sold by grocers. It also represents the fruit of justice, including the work of lawyers and police officers and community organizers and legislators.

The spirituality of work propels people to understand the Eucharist as their jobs made holy and to treat their jobs as an extension of the

Eucharist. "Not where I work," many people will sincerely reply. Such Christians have to realize that the gifts that come up the aisle at Mass, like the people who come through the doors of the church, are imperfect. Mediocrity, disinterest, laziness, dishonesty, and gossip detract from the wholeness of work and blemish the bread and wine on the offertory table.

But Christians take heart from believing that the world and its inhabitants have already been redeemed. Thus the Mass includes a Penitential Rite during which worshippers reflect on their faults and failings, yet also on the abiding mercy and forgiveness of our loving God.

The Unity of Worship and Work

The spirituality of work is somewhat idealistic in promoting a form of holiness in which work and worship come together, for work can be hectic and rough and not very amenable to acts of social justice. Liturgy too is often poorly celebrated, with little recognition that its meaning depends on how well the mystical body of Christ lives the Eucharist Monday through Saturday.

Nonetheless, there are many opportunities for strengthening the link between work and worship. For example, William Farley, a real estate developer in Hartford, Connecticut, starts with the image of his desk as an altar:

> I try to remember that all of us at Mass are concelebrating. Isn't it also possible that I can concelebrate the liturgy of my work with all the people around my desk—my partners and fellow employees? Once in a while I feel I am doing this in my company.

With some effort Christians might imagine their workplaces as chapels, if not cathedrals. They might try, however imperfectly, to regard their coworkers and customers as fellow worshippers. With a little creativity and a dose of patience workers are capable of devising simple ways to offer up and bless the ordinary, mundane labors of life and transform them into things of beauty.

The Prayer Over the Gifts, which contains the phrase "work of human hands" and is said during the Preparation of the Gifts, is often prayed silently. It would be a good practice, however, for presiders to make a point of reading the words aloud at times so that the full significance of this prayer can enter the minds and hearts of the workers in the pews.

Another likely place for improvement at Eucharist is the homily. As Fr. Dominic Grassi of St. Josaphat in Chicago, recounts:

> One Sunday I tried preaching about God in the workplace, and I realized how precious little I had to say because I am not in the workplace. Subsequently I invited some parishioners to discuss the topic over pizza and beer. The group now meets regularly.

When he began to meet regularly with parishioners, Grassi noticed a difference in his preaching. Recently, he reports, "a banker approached me after Mass, asking to register in the parish. He had never before heard in a church that his banking experience pertained to Scripture."

Specific occupations can be honored on specific Sundays or in conjunction with the feasts of patron saints. The art around the church could reflect the work of the worshippers. There might be places within the liturgy for workers, in written or spoken word, to reflect on their daily life—what in some denominations is called witnessing.

Perhaps the best way to improve the liturgy is for every worshipper to really attend to her or his neighbors, family members, and coworkers after Mass. Fr. John Flynn, for example, concluded a tour of his church in Chicago by asking the boys from a nearby Catholic high school: "What is the most important object in this church?" "The exit sign," one boy replied. With sarcasm, Flynn retorted: "And why do you suppose the exit sign is so important?" "Because," the student continued, "it shows us the direction in which to take the gospel."

"The Mass is ended. Go in peace to love and serve the Lord." Those words could be the most meaningful message in the whole Mass. Taken to heart, attended to in the fullest sense, and acted upon, those words can transform the world.

It is certainly not easy to practice a type of spirituality in which daily labor and liturgy come together. But even in the most hectic circumstances, people can deliberately consecrate their work and—in imperfect fashion—witness the image of the eucharistic Christ in their employees, coworkers, suppliers, customers, spouse, children, and neighbors.

As the Morning Offering prayer recognizes, people will not be conscious during the day that all their "works, joys and sufferings" are associated with the church's Eucharist. Instead, people will correctly be preoccupied hourly by details of the task at hand. But by regularly setting aside time for prayer and by regularly participating in the Eucharist, Christian workers, parents, students, and neighbors can meaningfully reinforce the unity of work and worship.

Sabbath Time

The spirituality of work is not a reckless assault against reflective disciplines, in favor of unmitigated and uninterrupted immersion in the world. In fact, the spirituality of work is predicated on methodically taking a step back in order to take two steps forward. Thus, an essential part of a spirituality of work is Sabbath time.

Sabbath time has been a social principle from the days of Moses. It is ironic then that something won with much difficulty in ancient Egypt is today given away so easily. Work is becoming an intoxicant—at least among a growing segment of the population. A professional can easily put in nearly fifty-four hours a week on the job. An owner of a small business is at work for almost sixty hours a week. The five o'clock dad is an endangered species. Of fathers with children under age six, almost forty percent are on the job more than fifty hours per week.

Trends in the economy often encourage companies to squeeze more out of salaried employees, routinely asking people to stay an extra hour or two. At the same time many people in middle management put in long hours because they don't have the job security they once enjoyed. In addition, information technology makes it difficult for today's workers to draw a distinct boundary between their private lives and their occupations. Work follows, accompanies, and even precedes them home. According to one survey, forty percent of North Americans contact their office each day of their vacation. When workers do carve out a little leisure time, their favorite activities are watching TV and going shopping, neither of which qualify as Sabbath time. It might be noted that both watching TV (indirectly) and shopping (directly), fuel the economy that requires people to spend more hours on the job.

The spirituality of work suggests one hour of Sabbath time a day, one Sabbath day a week, and optimally one Sabbath weekend a year for a retreat. For Christians, the weekly Sabbath day is Sunday. That first day of the week is set aside by social principle, not arbitrarily. To say that any day can be the Lord's Day is simply one more example of North American individualism.

Wholesale Sabbath-breaking has ruinous effects on culture. The shoddiness of many personal relationships today is a consequence of sins against time. True family life, true marital intimacy, and true friendship require time—away from the soccer match, the TV, the job, the shopping mall. Short of a major change in culture and the laws, the restoration of weekly Sabbath time will require countercultural efforts on the part of families.

The Sunday Sabbath begins with the liturgy, which brings the work of the week to the altar and carries the body and blood of Christ into the week that follows. The Sabbath cannot, however, be reduced to simply going to church. The whole day is an opportunity to refrain from acting upon the world and instead, to celebrate the grandeur and mystery of creation—especially God's most precious creation, humankind.

On the Sabbath Christians can recall the grand stories of liberation, including the story from ancient Egypt where working masses ended a seven-day-a-week slavery system. Full-time Christians share big meals on Sunday during which people sit around the table laughing and arguing. Of course, all family members help prepare for and clean up after such meals. Sunday is a day for reading and listening to music. For married couples, Sunday is a day for sex. (Other days are OK, too.)

Sabbath time—daily, weekly, and optimally an annual retreat—is essential to a spirituality that propels people into their work and sustains them as they fashion their homes, their neighborhoods, and their businesses into places that more closely resemble the kingdom of God.

4

The Virtue of Social Justice

> It grows increasingly true that the obligations of justice and love
> are fulfilled only if each person, contributing to the common
> good according to his [or her] own abilities and the needs of oth-
> ers, also promotes and assists the public and private institutions
> dedicated to bettering the conditions of human life.
>
> —*Pastoral Constitution on the Church in the Modern World*

"The term social justice frequently is used as a catch-all term for doing
good," says Ron Krietemeyer of Catholic Charities in St. Paul,
Minnesota. But social justice can have a much more precise meaning.

Krietemeyer gives this example: a woman owns a small business
and pays many of the workers the minimum wage. One day the business owner decides to increase the hourly wage by two dollars. This
is not an example of social justice, Krietemeyer explains. Assuming it
would not jeopardize the business, this is "an individual act of generosity and fairness. But it would not change the larger structures—the
labor market that keeps wages at the minimum level." In terms of
social justice, the business owner should get involved in her trade
association, trying "to raise wages in the whole industry or collectively advocating for a law that would set the minimum wage at a higher
level." Krietemeyer concludes, "Social justice is not about private individual acts. It is about collective actions aimed at transforming social
institutions and structures in order to achieve the common good."

Why spend time trying to define social justice? After all, hasn't the phrase gained such wide currency in the post-Vatican II church that everyone understands it? In fact, nearly a quarter of all the parishes in the Diocese of Buffalo, New York—to take only one example—have an official peace and justice committee. Nearly all Buffalo parishes have some regular outreach to the needy: a St. Vincent de Paul society, a food pantry, a clothing drive, an annual Crop walk, and more. Still, for all the talk about social justice in church circles, there is a realization that the practice of social justice is not nearly as effective as it might be. Perhaps it would not hurt to reexamine the virtue of social justice itself.

Fr. William Ferree, who died in 1985, greatly influenced an earlier generation of North American social thinkers with his commentaries on social justice. This virtue, Ferree explains, is easily confused with other virtues: charity or distributive justice, for example. The unique act of social justice, he says, is organization by like-minded people. The aim or outcome of social justice is improved policies or institutions. Ferree uses an example of a businessman who called a Christian radio program and said:

> I am trying to be a Christian at work but the tide is running against me. Business ethics have been reduced to "everybody's doing it." If I don't do some questionable things my competitor will, and I'll be out of business. I have a family to support, a home to maintain, food and clothing to buy.

The answer given on the radio program was, "Right is right even if nobody else does it. Wrong is wrong even if everybody does it." In Ferree's opinion, this was not helpful advice. The caller already knew right from wrong.

Ferree mentions three other inadequate responses: 1) do the best you can; 2) go ahead and behave like everyone else because under the principle of double effect it is not your primary intention to perpetuate evil; 3) quit your job. The man's only hope, Ferree explains, is to take the situation out of the realm of individual ethics. The businessman needs to understand the notion of social justice and then exercise some calculated Christian courage. He has to organize a group of fellow business people, either from his own company or from several companies. The group has to agree on certain codes of conduct, no matter how minimal the restraint. The group then has to institute that behavior in the industry.

This task is not as impossible as it might first seem. Here's an example: the printing business, with its use of chemicals, is responsible for a fair share of pollution. It also, by the nature of the business, depletes natural resources. One printing shop on the corner or another in the mall is helpless in addressing these issues. To make a unilateral change would only give an advantage to a competitor.

However, printers acting collectively through their trade association, the Printing Industries of America, have made big improvements. Starting in the Great Lakes area, where nearly half of all the nation's printing is done, the trade association has devised policies for the purchase and use of raw materials and recycled paper, as well as for the storage and disposal of photo chemicals, waste inks, and cleaning solvents. The trade association got the cooperation of some government agencies, unions, and several large customers of the printers. By agreeing together to change the way they do business, the participating print shops have made a major contribution to recycling and toward the elimination of pollution.

Over the past twenty years and more, pro-abortion resolutions have been introduced in committees and assemblies of several professional associations and at various levels in labor unions. In some situations these resolutions are mostly symbolic; in others they allow the organization to lobby against restrictions on abortions and to file friend-of-the-court briefs on behalf of abortion rights. To protest such resolutions, some Christians have discontinued their membership in their association. Other professionals and union members, however, have organized like-minded colleagues and garnered enough support to reverse the pro-abortion policies and at least get the union or association to take no position on the issue.

Racial steering and block busting are abuses that occur in the real estate, mortgage, and insurance industries, and have plagued East Coast and Great Lakes cities for decades. These practices have greatly contributed to wholesale resegregation in Buffalo, Philadelphia,

Cleveland, Detroit, and many other cities, and they supply a third example of an "inside" approach to social justice. Many individual real estate agents, even some who were educated in Catholic schools, have proven unable to resist the temptation of getting a commission by immoral means. Meanwhile, even the most sophisticated community organizations have only been able to pressure one or another realtor, without actually stopping resegregation.

Some progress is made, however, when realtors get together and take action through their professional boards. The Southwest Suburban Board of Realtors in the Chicago area, for example, now sends testers of various racial and ethic backgrounds into the offices of their own members. The board penalizes any broker or firm that considers race and ethnicity when talking to customers. The board also requires its members to periodically attend fair housing classes.

Perfect social justice is not, of course, achieved through one program. The situation in many neighborhoods has come to such an impasse that only by affirmatively marketing the benefits of neighborhood integration will fuller justice be achieved. Under the letter of the law, the boards of realtors do not think their members can promote the positives of integration. Thus, the issue awaits more people who will organize programs and institutions to improve fair housing practices.

The Insider Approach

Notice there are no picket lines or other means of extraordinary protest in these examples. While protest might play a role in setting the stage for social justice, as it certainly did in the real estate example, the two are not to be equated. This suggests a distinction between "outsiders" and "insiders." The outsider, who in recent years has seemed to serve as the model for social justice, is certainly interested in change but often not overly concerned with how to implement reform. The insider, on the other hand, is the one who must attend to the institutional details for reform. The prophets of peace and justice are desperately needed. Making social justice a constitutive dimension of living the gospel, however, requires a more lucid explanation of the insider's role. The late Lawrence Ragan, a communications executive from Chicago, explains the distinction in personal terms:

There are the insiders and the outsiders. Two kinds of people. Two ways of looking at life. Two ways of making things happen.

The outsiders raise hell. They demonstrate; they organize marches. They issue reports that excoriate the establishment, challenge the status quo, appeal to all who thirst for justice.

The insiders? Often dull. The insiders speak a different language: they know the tax tables, the zoning variations, the assessment equalizers, the square-foot cost to educate the kids. You'll find them on the school board, city government, on the village board. Ordinarily not word people, they have mastered the art of the platitude.

Outsiders are often wild. At first, they don't seem to make sense. The first black kids who sat at a lunch counter and refused to move were outsiders. The first marchers to Selma were outsiders. Surely it was an outsider who first proposed the shocking idea that the generic "he" is a sexist word. Dorothy Day, who in the 1950s stopped Manhattan traffic to protest atom bomb tests, was an outsider.

Please God, let us always have outsiders and give me the grace, in my better moments, to know how to be one. But I'm torn because I want to be an insider too. The insiders resist the first answer that comes to them: they have heard it before. They are offended when they see the world's complexities reduced to slogans shouted into a microphone or preached at a town hall meeting. They are saddened when they hear someone argue that God is on his or her side, and they wonder why God doesn't speak so clearly to them.

Sometimes you've got to feel sorry for the insiders. When they win, few know of their victory. When they go wrong, their mistakes are branded as evil. Often they share the goals of the outsider but continue to say, "things aren't that simple."

The world is filled with people who like to feel they are right. Insiders are not always certain they are right. They are unhappy when they must resist the simplicities of popular sloganeering. So when we tip our hats to the outsiders, as so often we must, let's not do so with such vigor that we fail to give two cheers to the insider.

The insider approach to social justice, it becomes obvious, requires plenty of prudent compromising. Says Peggy O'Brien Steinfels of *Commonweal* magazine, it is an approach that "looks pale" and less pure to the prophets who often have the microphone. Yet in Scripture, Steinfels explains, "the prophet is a necessary and corrective exception, not the norm." The best way for most Christians to get involved "is to be more intelligently, more skillfully, more devotedly political." We need to remember, she concludes, that the purpose of getting involved "is to build up those institutions and associations and ways of life that will create and maintain the social infrastructure that so many individuals and communities are sorely lacking."

John Mahoney, SJ, reminds us that the classic Judeo-Christian prophets, in addition to calling people to task, were capable, from time to time, of offering "comfort and consolation." So too today's prophets could be more sympathetic to the insider. The biblical prophets, who spoke from the outside, often found "room and recognition for others in society who are deeply concerned about how human beings behave and relate to each other." Today's prophets, instead of relying too "strongly on the emotion of moral indignation," might consider lowering "the volume of denunciation" to avoid "moral bullying."

Christian insiders are the ones who are sensitive to style, tone, and basic posture. The insider is aware of failures in the economy, in healthcare delivery, in education, and more. Yet the insider respects the basic ethos of business, hospitals, colleges, courts of law, and other institutions. The insider is capable of praising the successes of one system or another. From time to time, the insider is willing to pay moral compliments to government, labor, business, the arts, and social service. The insider, for example, knows to criticize unemployment or low wages. But the insider has also learned how to describe the creation of steady jobs in terms of social virtue.

None of this is to imply that the outsider is unnecessary. Many great changes in history are direct byproducts of an outsider's protest. The fall of communism, for example, was mostly accomplished by outsiders. The communism example, on the other hand, also illustrates that outsiders often cannot carry social change to its conclusion.

While studying the changes in Eastern Europe, Andrew Nagorski interviewed many of the outsiders who toppled communism. He quickly became sensitive to "the perils of the transformation of dissidents into establishment politicians, from outsiders to insiders." For example, Nagorski claims that many of the problems Lech Walesa experienced as president of Poland were related to "the general difficulty of making the psychological switch from the politics of resistance to normal democratic politics."

Nagorski mentions other protesters against communism who had difficulty building democratic institutions once they were in charge. He concludes:

> The qualities required of dissidents proved in many cases to be the opposite of those required of political leaders in a democratic system. All dissidents had to have a stubborn, unrelenting quality....But a political leader who is completely uncompromising and prone to see others as conspirators can hardly be effective....
> It may have been precisely because the tradition of rebellion and dissent was so strong in Poland [and other Eastern European countries] that the process of constructing a workable new political system proved so difficult.

Full-time Social Justice

While it is true that the phrase "social justice" is now heard regularly in church circles, the impression is often created that people best advance justice and peace by stepping outside of their ordinary roles as business people, professionals, civil servants, or active union members in order to volunteer for a church-designed social action program. Such an idea clearly departs from mainstream Christian social thought, which regards the exercise of social justice as essentially the service performed within one's professional and occupational milieu. The recent preoccupation with the role of the outsider as the model of social action can inadvertently distract ordinary Christians from the apostolic potential that lies at the core of their civic, family, and occupational lives.

Veteran Catholic activist Ed Marciniak states the problem in strong language:

Among many church leaders and their staffs there lingers an abiding disdain for those Christians who work inside the political and economic system and a predilection for those who are stationed outside or against the system. Many of the church's civil servants (priests, religious and laity who are full-timers in the parish or diocesan office) operate with a built-in bias. From the periphery of economic and political institutions they tend to stand in judgment and condemnation, not knowing how to commend, encourage, or support the insiders, those businessmen, professional women and men, union leaders who are persons of integrity and allergic to injustice.

Steve Rall, who directs parish social ministry for the Diocese of Lansing, Michigan, puts it succinctly: "We church employees spend ninety-five percent of our time trying to get five percent of the people engaged in social ministry as we define it, while ninety-five percent of the people are on the cutting edge without any support from us."

Who Speaks for the Church?

It is presumed in rectories, in newspaper columns, in television studios, and in the minds of many Christians that the church is present in the world when bishops or other church employees speak on public policy. It is not as well recognized, however, that the church humanizes the world when Christians who are insiders to society bear the burden of sustaining and improving political, economic, and cultural institutions. Bishops, priests, and other church employees must preach the gospel of peace and justice. According to Vatican II, however, it is insiders who, through their vocations in professions, occupations, and states in life, give shape and form to a more just and peaceful society.

This is not a tidy proposition. Tested models for how the church is to understand and act in the world while remaining true to itself are only emerging. Different people in different neighborhoods or legislatures can entertain different notions of a church in service to the world. There is some room for different styles. A Vatican II ecclesiology, however, is predicated on a lay-centered model.

To implement the Vatican II vision of a church with a worldly vocation, all baptized Christians must become more confident and competent. They must grow in their dedication to their jobs, their families, and their neighborhoods. They must also, through reflection, better appreciate that their daily dedication, in itself, is Christian witness. Full-time Christians must believe that ordinary work done in exemplary fashion is the church being a church after the church service.

Church employees can make a significant contribution to helping workaday Christians be confident and competent agents of justice. Those church employees might start by presenting Catholic social teaching in less careless, bureaucratic, and partisan ways. In particular, church employees ought to refrain from quoting the Bible and papal encyclicals in a fundamentalist way, implying that Jesus or Christian social teaching has one specific answer to a very knotty social or political problem. For example, there is nothing in Scripture or in papal writings that directly speaks to issues of pollution and safety at large-scale hog farms in the Midwest. Yet an employee of the church recently thought he needed to vindicate his lobbying of a state legislature on these issues by claiming the support of John Paul II's encyclical *On Social Concerns*. This church employee seemed to imply that Christians cannot make informed decisions about farm legislation unless they quote the Bible or encyclicals by chapter and verse.

Ordinary Christians are likewise dissuaded from the Vatican II ideal of competent and confident laity when church employees speak as if they represent all Christians in a city, state, or church jurisdiction. For example, there are thirty-two Catholic Conferences in the United States that lobby legislatures on behalf of bishops. When it comes to support of or opposition to a particular funding bill, however, the employees of these Conferences are in the habit of saying—to the press and to legislators—that they represent the Catholic position. Except on a very clear-cut moral matter (certainly not hog farming), it is quite possible that sincere and informed Christians in the legislature and among voters have a position different from the Conference lobbyist.

Or take the matter of church employees using nouns like diocese or church interchangeably with themselves. It is one thing for the director of a chancery peace and justice office to write an op/ed letter on public housing. It says something else, however, when the letter claims to be "the position of the church...which knows the future of public housing." What conclusion is to be drawn by an informed Christian in city hall, in the department of Housing and Urban Development, in an urban studies institute of a university, in a public housing tenants' group? Must their positions agree with the diocesan employee in order for them to be in harmony with the church?

As a first step in learning how to impart social teaching, church employees might spend more time listening to the wisdom of health-care professionals, lawyers, homemakers, civil servants, elected officials, and others. Granted, these are not mutually exclusive categories. Many excellent healthcare professionals are also employees of the church; many accomplished homemakers are employees of the church. But how many annual meetings of official church organizations in the country—to say nothing of groups that meet at the chancery or in a parish hall—feature non-church employees on the program? An unscientific survey of advertisements for seventy of those annual meetings turns up only four non-church employees as speakers. And where is there a conference at which ordinary Christian leaders talk about their insider efforts on behalf of peace and justice on the job and in the community? If such forums are available, they are not being advertised in parish bulletins and Christian magazines or newspapers.

The Right to Organize a Union

Theology textbooks in the 1950s always demonstrated the virtue of social justice with the Catholic doctrine on unions. (Not all religious traditions share this doctrine.) It is unfashionable today to use the example of unions to illustrate the virtue of social justice. Yet Catholic social teaching, so "full of grandiose terms," says Kevin Clarke of *U.S. Catholic* magazine, started with two humble words: "worker and union." According to Clarke, the modern rendition of Catholic social morality began in 1891 with

> Pope Leo XIII's *Rerum Novarum* [which] asserted the special dignity of human labor and defended the right of workers to form unions, the right to collective bargaining, the right, yes, even to strike....This focus [is] the foundation of all the social teaching that has followed.

There are several points of view on most moral issues. As with other moral issues, Catholic social teaching has assessed the various points of view regarding unions and has reached some conclusions. As with other doctrines there certainly are Catholics in good conscience who take exception to the teaching on unions. It is not correct, however, to say that according to Catholic teaching there are two sides to this topic.

The basic Catholic doctrine on unions is this: after thinking about the common good, workers are morally entitled to decide in favor or against a union without the maternal or paternal interference of their employer and without any harassment from union organizers. Because Catholic social thought has never accepted the notion that wages and working conditions can be left entirely to the free market, it is not considered a failure in management if workers vote for a union. Likewise, Catholic doctrine, with its picture of an organic society, never considers affiliates of national or regional unions to be outside third parties.

Catholic doctrine does not say that every place of employment needs to be unionized. Nor does Catholic doctrine say managers cannot bargain tough. Catholic doctrine does not imply that every union action is advisable. Nor does Catholic doctrine vouch for the wisdom of one or another union official, as it likewise refrains from endorsing one or another manager or executive. Catholic doctrine simply insists that workers are intelligent enough and morally entitled to make their own decision about forming a union—even if that decision seems unwise to the employer, who may indeed be a sincere Christian. Further, Catholic doctrine is convinced that a union movement—always in need of reform—is indispensable in facilitating virtue in a modern economy, in distributing the output of production among the whole populace, and in safeguarding workplaces where people can enjoy dignity.

Mary Ann Glendon, of Harvard Law School, nudges her fellow neoconservatives to embrace this last point. "Unions are important mediating associations," she says. It is incorrect to "think unions are fine for Poland, but not the United States."

There are corollaries to the basic Catholic doctrine on unions. Companies or institutions cannot retain union-busting consultants, nor, naturally, is a Catholic allowed to hold a decision-making position in a union-busting law firm or public relations firm. Companies or institutions cannot, under Catholic doctrine, hire so-called permanent replacement workers.

Further, according to people like the late Cardinal John O'Connor of New York City, Catholics are not allowed to cross a picket line during a just strike or legitimate strike. O'Connor made this point to a benefit committee of a Catholic institution planning a golf outing at a country club, which at the time was the target of a strike. "I unconditionally disapprove [of Catholics] using facilities where workers are on strike," O'Connor said. To "knowingly and deliberately" cross a legitimate picket line, according to O'Connor, is to express "contempt for collective bargaining." If Catholics took O'Connor's explanation of their doctrine to heart, it seems obvious that strikes would be even rarer than they are today and labor/management negations would more frequently remain on track.

Finally, Catholic social teaching reminds managers and employees of Catholic institutions that when it comes to the doctrine on unions, the church should be exemplary. Sadly, the entire tradition of Catholic social thought appears hypocritical when, for example, a religious order allows one of its hospitals or agencies to retain a union-busting firm.

Social Holiness

Some commentators are of the opinion that the term "social justice" is either so loosely used or so tied to a particular ideology that it should be abandoned. The intriguing phrase "social holiness" has been suggested as a substitute.

But debate about a name is not the real issue. The challenge is to step back for a moment from particular issues like nuclear disarmament, opposition to abortion, or support for a living wage. What's needed instead is reflection on the habit or virtue that Christians must acquire in order to live the gospel in its fullness on the job, around the home, and in the community. It is a virtue that disposes a Christian to look for potential leaders among the people he or she meets during the week. It is a virtue that prompts a Christian to share their vision, no matter how modest, at workplace meetings or around the home. It is a virtue that enables a Christian to attract like-minded people to projects in the community or at the office.

It is a virtue that resembles charity and draws upon a person's generosity, compassion, perseverance, and willingness to act. This particular virtue, however, takes a step beyond charitable giving. It alerts a Christian to opportunities for social change. It is associated with righteous anger, prudence, sophistication, and courage. This virtue is also sufficiently associated with humility so that it can, as appropriate, recognize the legitimacy of differing positions. This virtue gives a Christian the ability to look beyond the immediate purposes of a group toward the common good. As warranted, it gives a Christian the confidence to critique his or her group, while upholding its original mission.

This virtue is manifest as two or four or a thousand Christians and other sympathetic people get together to study a situation, to strategize over remedies and, most crucially, to act for improvements. Their collective behavior is directed not as much toward an immediate problem as toward a policy change that will diminish the problem in the future.

Call this virtue social justice or social holiness. By whatever name, it is not possible to be a responsible, full-time Christian in the twenty-first century without acquiring and exercising this unique virtue. In summary, here are some of the traits of the virtue of social justice:

• The virtue of social justice is a collective virtue. It can only be practiced by two or more people.

• The distinct act of social justice is getting like-minded people together.

• The purpose or target of such organization is improved policies or institutions. This means that social justice is addressed to institutions not, as with the virtue of charity, to individuals. Thus, social justice deals with the cause of a problem, not so much with the related and perhaps temporary consequences of that problem.

• To achieve its purpose, the practice of social justice might include protest, but protest alone is not social justice. It is quite possible to practice social justice without using a picket sign, without sloganeering, without raised voices. This does not mean that social justice is a pleasant virtue. Change always means conflict, friction, challenge. At the same time, social justice does not "stand on principle." It is effective because it knows the value of compromise.

Each group practicing social justice knows that its opponents can likely be groups and institutions equally committed to social justice. All social justice endeavors are, by the nature of the virtue, imperfect. In other words, social justice is a this-worldly virtue. There is no need for social justice in heaven, where only love abides. By tomorrow, today's social justice efforts must be improved upon. There is never enough.

5

The Sacrament of Neighborhood

In our times a special obligation binds us to make ourselves the neighbor of absolutely every person, and of actively helping [that person] when he [or she] comes across our path, whether he [or she] be an old person abandoned by all, a foreign laborer unjustly looked down upon, a refugee, a child...or a hungry person who disturbs our conscience by recalling the voice of the Lord: "As long as you did it for one of the least of these, you did it for me."

—*Pastoral Constitution on the Church in the Modern World*

To the census taker or to a topographer a neighborhood is addresses, coordinates, lines, boundaries, and landmarks. Real neighborhood identity is more fluid, however, for a variety of economic, emotional, intellectual, and political reasons. Competing interests often battle over what an area should be called or how far neighborhood boundaries stretch. There are arguments too over what makes for a good neighborhood and what constitutes a bad neighborhood. As Alan Plattus of Yale University has discovered, "some of the things that make communities good places to live have less to do with the state of the plumbing and more to do with the relationships that are formed." Thus, simply moving to a new locale doesn't guarantee a better neighborhood or a better life.

Neighborhoods, whose names and identifying characteristics are indeed fluid, can be defined as geographically based support systems. Their intended purpose is to help people negotiate their way in the larger metropolis. Neighborhoods include libraries, restaurants, churches, and clubs as well as bankers, activists, merchants, and the unemployed. The meaning of neighborhood transcends sidewalks and curbs, street signs and pavement. Consequently, neighborhoods can be urban or suburban, rural or small town.

Christians are interested in neighborhoods because their God is revealed through a community of people. Or, as expressed by John Haughey, SJ: "The everyday noise of the city block is teeming with the word of God. The neighborhood invites us to partner with God in making the broken more whole." With that understanding, full-time Christians do not regard their neighborhood as merely a social or geographical phenomenon. It is, to them, a sacred community.

Catholics in particular have a sensibility for neighborhood life because of the Catholic emphasis on the dogma of the Incarnation. The circumstances of the Bethlehem event remind us that our extraordinary God is revealed in the ordinary. The Catholic imagination is able to see Christ around the neighborhood in the same way he once was found in Joseph's carpenter shop and on the streets of Nazareth. Particularly for Catholics, the Incarnation means that everyone and everything is a potential sacrament, a source of grace "to those who have eyes to see and ears to hear."

Of course, like other sacraments, the neighborhood both reveals and disguises what it contains. God isn't gloriously reigning from a throne on the boulevard. It takes faith to see God in the neighborhood; in some neighborhoods that's easier than in others.

Because of their sacramental way of appropriating God, says Fr. Andrew Greeley, "Catholics can be expected to have an interest in studying the social structure of neighborhoods and reflecting on the religious meaning of the neighborhood phenomenon." Greeley explains how neighborhoods foster certain virtues:

Human beings…are predisposed to informal, intimate, affectionate, trusting relationships.…[But] such relationships are not without ambivalence or suspicion, for the basic human flaw is fear....When you provide humans with the structures and the motivations for overcoming their distrust sufficiently [they can] give themselves in affectionate vulnerability one to another.

The neighborhood is one institution that allows for appropriate public vulnerability, for conviviality. For at the same time the neighborhood exposes strangers to one another, it also protects "the dignity and the freedom of the individual person...[which] can only [happen] when as much social and political power as possible is maintained at the lowest possible level in the society." The neighborhood, Greeley concludes, is an excellent example of "the Catholic principle of subsidiarity [which] can be articulated in the somewhat less poetic but more precise slogan, no bigger than necessary."

Parish Is Neighborhood

For Catholics, a parish is an extension of the Christian life celebrated inside the sanctuary and—at least in some places—the neighborhood is regarded as an extension of the parish. For example, in some parts of Philadelphia and Chicago, real estate agents refer to a neighborhood by using the name of the local church: "I've got a listing in St. Ben's," or "I just sold a two-flat in Fives or Queens" (Five Holy Martyrs or Queen of the Universe).

The Catholic imagination is capable of regarding everything within parish boundaries as sacred space. Shops, homes, apartment buildings, union halls, ethnic clubs, and even taverns are all part of the link between parish and neighborhood. In fact, the pastoral equivalence of the parish and its neighborhood is taken for granted in some interpretations of canon law, diocesan policies, and parish guidelines. A Catholic pastor, for example, frequently serves as the chaplain (officially or unofficially) to any college, shelter, union hall, or civic association within his boundaries.

Likewise, parish facilities are routinely available to groups in the neighborhood—provided there is no conflict with a parish function. In fact, by Catholic tradition a parish must serve all within its boundaries, regardless of religious affiliation. This link between the parish and the neighborhood (a link also made by some mosques, synagogues, and Protestant churches) goes a long way toward humanizing a city and making its citizens more familiar to one another.

It is curious then that Catholic parishes have lately forsaken the practice of enforcing geographic boundaries. One bulletin, for example, boasts: "The majority of people who come here do so from all across the diocese and participate in different ways." At another urban parish the annual report notes that ninety-nine percent of the worshippers live one mile or more from the church building. A leader at another church introduced himself by saying he lives six miles away from the church building, highlighting the non-geographic flavor of that particular Catholic church.

It is interesting too that literature and signs in many Catholic parishes prefer the words "church," "community," and even "congregation" rather than the word "parish." But the concept of parish is really more inclusive than the concept of congregation. A congregation refers to the people who come through the doors of a church, no matter where they live in relation to the church building. A parish refers to the area within a square mile or more of the church building—no matter who lives and works in that area.

The trend to think about parish life in non-geographic terms—a trend that is similar to the way Protestant churches have long been organized—does have advantages. It enables Catholics to find a style of worship that is enriching to them, and may motivate some pastoral teams to improve their preaching, their music, and their hospitality. It allows parishes to recruit talent and money from outside normal boundaries. It keeps some Catholic schools open and, by allowing people from the suburbs to return to their old neighborhood, it sustains some ethnic customs or some clubs.

On the other hand, non-geographic parishes can potentially undermine elements that are distinct and valuable to a neighborhood parish: for example, the sacramental imagination attuned to street level surroundings and an experience of community based on real turf.

The Particular and the Universal

The Catholic sacrament of neighborhood, with its parishes and parochial schools, is sometimes accused of fostering exclusivity and narrowness. The Catholic ghetto, the argument goes, impedes Catholics from becoming open-minded, racially tolerant, culturally assimilated, and sophisticated in all manner.

It is true that under the leadership of its pastor, more than one parish has organized to keep a neighborhood segregated. It is true that students from a Catholic school have shouted vile racial and ethnic slurs at students from other schools. It is true that some unions, led by Catholics formed in a parish environment, have systematically kept people of an ethnic or racial group out of a trade or occupation. It is true that some Catholic realtors practice racial steering, some Catholic bankers and insurance brokers condone redlining (a form of racial segregation), some Catholic public servants do not afford full civil rights and human dignity to gays, women, blacks, Asian-Americans, Jewish-Americans, Arab-Americans, the elderly, the poor, immigrants—take your pick.

On the other hand, when it comes to voting, Catholics are more likely than the general population to back social policies that redistribute resources to the disadvantaged, to new arrivals, to the poor. By every attitudinal survey, Catholics are more tolerant of others and their lifestyles than the general population, and the tolerance quotient increases for each year a Catholic spent in a Catholic school. Catholics are well-known for their involvement in labor unions, community organizations, civic causes, charitable endeavors, and civil rights campaigns. Some of the most talented artists, filmmakers, singers, and poets in the country were educated in Catholic schools. Catholics (including the numerous Catholics who have recently immigrated from Mexico, the Philippines, and elsewhere) are now the most educated and wealthiest gentile denomination.

So yes, the particularity of the Catholic neighborhood doesn't always form responsible citizens. In some cases it reinforces prejudice. But overwhelmingly the Catholic ghetto, by giving people a secure base, actually propels them into a wider arena and gives them the skills and confidence to extend opportunity to others. Each neighborhood is a mix of the city of God and the city of man. The Catholic strategy is to bless the neighborhood (or the trade union or the political machine), warts and all—to bless it and encourage its potential.

At its best, explains Cardinal Francis George, OMI, of Chicago, Christianity and its expression in the Catholic neighborhood prepares people for universalism. Beginning with the parable of the Good Samaritan and continuing through all the lessons learned in the parish and parochial school, Christians are taught to be "inclusive neighbors." The parish and other Christian institutions, George continues, bring a theology and a tradition to the neighborhood. The church—sometimes in regular rituals and sometimes in special programs—makes "differences public so that they can be shared to create a richer unity."

The Catholic experience also stands apart from what today goes by the name "pluralism" or "diversity" but is really a false tolerance. In some schools and businesses diversity is supposedly celebrated—but only if what is brought into public view is of the least common denominator. Real differences are expected to be kept private. Catholicism, by contrast, persists in its peculiar pageants and processions and gestures and customs. And Catholicism, in true tolerance, welcomes to the public square the fasts and feasts, the art and literature of other denominations, other religions, other traditions.

There is a genius to neighborhood life. It provides local attachments and a safe harbor that forcefully launches Catholics into the mainstream without severing their compassionate roots. This remarkable North American liberation practice is repeated as each Catholic immigrant group makes its way to Texas, Colorado, California, New York, and other points on the continent.

The Neighborhood Lost and Found

Over the years, of course, the importance of neighborhood life was neglected by both public policy planners and by ordinary residents. Beginning as early as 1950, many neighborhood communities were literally destroyed in the name of progress. Urban neighborhoods were bulldozed and paved over with expressways, and cleared for hospital parking lots, university dorms, and sports arenas. From the mid-1980s through the 1990s, a wave of parish closings swept over cities situated on the Great Lakes and Atlantic coast. In the past forty years the Catholic population of Cleveland, Ohio for example, has declined by nearly fifty percent. In Chicago the decline was over thirty percent, off-set only by significant immigration from Mexico.

The trend since 1950 has been for families to locate in the suburbs. But there too neighborhood life has suffered as communities have lost or failed to establish their identity in the sprawl of malls, industrial parks, and housing tracts.

Recently, however, neighborhoods are enjoying something of an intellectual and practical revival. Several cities along the Atlantic coast and on the Great Lakes are witnessing development of their down-town and inner rim areas, thanks in part to young workers who desire a neighborhood experience. The decline in city population on the shores of the Great Lakes and the Atlantic Ocean began to level off in 1990. Some older cities are actually increasing their population. As early as the 1980s, says Ed Marciniak of the Institute of Urban Life, social policy planners and others began to understand that "self-conscious neighborhoods are among the most powerful energizers of urban revitalization."

The dynamics of today's revitalization vary from place to place. In one area the change is dramatic; in another it proceeds slowly. Yet neighborhood renewal is unmistakably occurring in Chicago, Baltimore, Cincinnati, Columbus, Denver, Indianapolis, and many other places. Every indication says the revitalization trend will continue and spread. In fact, scores of suburbs are redesigning their Main Streets to give residents the ambiance and amenities of an old world neighborhood. Even today's workplaces, reports Malcolm Gladwell of the *New Yorker*, are being designed to foster a social milieu patterned on neighborhoods. In today's businesses social knowledge is a primary asset. So rather than have managers sequestered from shipping clerks, the office as neighborhood puts in proximity people who seemingly don't have much in common with one another.

Today's revitalization is sometimes called gentrification, but the full story includes more than just yuppies remodeling lofts. It includes medical professionals—nurses, technicians, and researchers—who desire homes near a hospital complex. It includes information and service workers who find a walk to work appealing and so have abandoned the suburbs. It includes Russian immigrants who rehabitate buildings along a subway route. It includes Chinese immigrants who overspill a small Chinatown.

Today's revitalized neighborhoods are to a significant degree racially, ethnically, and economically integrated. The new neighborhoods are often dominated by mixed uses, where residential and commercial developments exist side by side.

And so many neighborhoods are experiencing a second spring, to judge by bricks and plywood, by public school enrollment figures, and by real estate prices. But amid the redevelopment, questions abound. Will the elderly and poor be displaced? Will venerable neighborhood institutions, like churches, survive if the new pioneers don't participate? Will the neighborhood eventually lose its attractive heterogeneous character? In other words, is it possible for a neighborhood to be simultaneously rehabited in a physical sense and neglected in another sense?

Because neighborhoods, in a sacramental sense, are really sets of relationships, neighborhoods are neglected when people simply quit relating to one another. Sadly, this neglect is too often happening in villages, large cities, towns, and rural areas. Too many neighborhoods have suffered from a surplus of building contractors and a shortage of visionaries. A neighborhood is not great because of its historic buildings, its unique architecture, or its commercial economy. A neighborhood is not great simply because it overlooks a river or a lake. A neighborhood is not great simply because it contains a university, a hospital, a transportation center, or a five-star restaurant.

A neighborhood's greatness arises from its hospitality to immigrants, to refugees seeking a new life, to students and workers, to the elderly and dispossessed, to young parents, and to the poor. From an unlikely mixture of neighborhood characters come poets, taxi drivers, teachers, and citizens. Neighborhoods are the incubators of culture and civilization. The neighborhood is the place where women and men come to make their way in the world. As relationships are nurtured and respected, a true neighborhood gives life to the next generation.

Community Organizations

In a Vatican II vision, the church normally acts upon the world as Christian laity join with like-minded people at work and in society to improve procedures, policies, laws, and institutions. Sometimes it is also necessary for the church as an institution to address the world. This is best done in dialogue with the world, though there are occasions when the institutional church should take a prophetic stance.

In the past thirty years the institutional church—at least in the United States—has gone overboard on issuing prophetic statements. Many church bodies (Catholic, Protestant, and ecumenical) have become irrelevant because they incessantly claim to speak "for the church," but in fact speak only for church employees.

Unfortunately, says Msgr. George Higgins, after Vatican II the justice and peace mission of the church "has tended to be a bit too clerical, too institutional or, if you will, too churchy." Higgins advises church leaders to "review our justice and peace policies and programs...to make sure they are adequately oriented toward forming authentic and autonomous lay leaders who will exercise their apostolate, not in and through church organizations, but in their secular occupations."

This shortsightedness may not be so new. Back in the 1920s Robert Woods warned against grand gestures:

> The rising tide of interest on the part of the church in social problems will simply lead to vague and scattered efforts in connection with this or that....It is quite easy to get into the position of the schoolgirl writing home and underlining every word. The net effect is the same as if there had been no emphasis at all.

Woods was not advising the institutional church to retreat from the world. When the church does act as an institution, "the true point of attack" should, however, be the local neighborhood, he said.

> This is also where the structural up-building of society has to begin. This is the distinctive unit and organ of social reconstruction. The neighborhood is the very pith and core and kernel and marrow of organic democracy....The neighborhood is thus the first unit of measurement for the progress of the kingdom of God....
>
> The sad fact about the church...is not so much that it is not informed about great [economic issues or municipal affairs or national legislation], or even about broader, public moral problems....The serious thing is that practically every Christian church

in the entire country is allowing itself to remain in the attitude of a divisive, disintegrating, influence...in its neighborhood, in the local community, for whose democratic progress it stands in the most solemn of all conceivable responsibilities.

According to civic activist Gregory Pierce of Chicago, the church has a role to play in getting neighbors

into public relationships, holding one another accountable, making meaningful deals, offering real support. It is not enough that neighbors know one another's first names, or that they nod their heads to one another in the grocery. It is not enough that neighbors like one another; they must learn to respect one another.

Respectful public relationships, Pierce continues, are forged in community organizations, among other places. A community organization

gives Christians an opportunity to carry out their theological beliefs in a real and efficacious manner by providing the opportunity for theological reflection on the connection between individual interests and public life, between religion and the world, between the parish and the neighborhood.

Today there are thousands of community organizations in cities, towns, suburbs, and rural areas. Many of them are affiliated with and partially funded by local parishes and by regional or national judicatories. There are also a half-dozen national networks of community organizations, the oldest and the best of which is the Industrial Areas Foundation, founded in the 1930s by Saul Alinsky, with headquarters now in Chicago.

Parishes are almost by definition supporters of community organizations, as many of them realize. A parish's institutional membership in a community organization will likely protect and enhance the parish's environment as the community organization combats crime, deteriorated housing, and the like. Such membership also helps to fulfill the justice and peace obligation incumbent upon every Christian institution. These are reasons enough for belonging to a community organization.

There is also the possibility that through participation in some of the better community organizations parish leaders will return to their parish groups with increased competency and renewed enthusiasm. For example, by using techniques taught by the Industrial Areas Foundation, one parish in Brooklyn increased its weekly collection by thirty-five percent; another by two-hundred-thirty percent in one year. A case study by the National Pastoral Life Center found that ninety percent of parishes receiving a diocesan subsidy were able to nearly or completely eliminate that subsidy after participating for three years in an Industrial Areas Foundation community organization.

Community organizations, like churches, can of course become isolated from the wider scene. In the day-to-day struggle it is easy to forget that every neighborhood-based initiative is inherently limited. No aggregate of local institutions can wield enough power to adequately address cultural trends that are impinging on family life today, for example.

The basic strategy of Saul Alinsky, who began organizing in Chicago's Back of the Yards neighborhood in the 1930s, assumed "that the neighborhood contained within it a number of vital organizations," explains John McKnight of Northwestern University.

> The basic Alinsky approach emphasized organizing in the consumer mode by assembling preexisting organizations into a kind of dense pack and propelling this aggregate toward a visible local decision-making structure to force it to do what the neighborhood wanted.

Today, however, each neighborhood is part of a global economy and a regional, if not national, polity. The traditional, umbrella-like, confrontation-prone community organization is not sufficiently pliable or sophisticated enough to deal with its complex milieu.

More than ever before, parishes and their community organizations must connect their local interests and resources with other institutions in the city, the diocese, and the nation. The principle of local subsidiarity must be balanced by the principle of global solidarity. Parish and neighborhood leaders are finding wisdom in the words of John Wesley: "The world is my parish; the parish is not my world."

6

The Principle of Subsidiarity

A few years ago a board game called Limbo was popular—briefly—among the generation of Catholics that straddled the Second Vatican Council. As in Trivial Pursuit, players had to "fill in the blank." For example, a Limbo player might have to "name the Catholic social principle used by economist E.F. Schumacher to illustrate his notion of small is beautiful." The correct answer is subsidiarity (from the Latin *subsidium*, to help or aid).

Most of the themes of Catholic social theory can be understood in relation to this key concept. Subsidiarity was given its classic formulation, albeit in arcane language, by Pope Pius XI in 1931:

> It is indeed true, as history clearly shows, that owing to the change in social conditions, much that was formerly done by small bodies can nowadays be accomplished only by large organizations. Nevertheless...it is an injustice and a grave evil and a disturbance of right order to transfer to the larger and higher collectivity functions which can be performed and provided for by lesser and subordinate bodies. Inasmuch as every social activity should, by its very nature, prove a help to members of the body social, it should never destroy or absorb them.

The United States Catholic bishops, in their pastoral letter *Economic Justice for All*, update the principle in these words:

In the principle of subsidiarity, Catholic social teaching has long stressed the importance of small and intermediate-sized communities or institutions for the exercise of moral responsibility. These mediating structures link the individual to society as a whole in a way that gives people greater freedom and power to act.

In Catholic social thought, explains Mary Ann Glendon, "the subsidiarity principle says that no social task should be performed by a larger institution than the smallest one that can handle the job adequately." In other words, Catholic philosophy celebrates "the mediating institutions of civil society...that fill the social space between individuals and the huge mega structures of the market and the state: families, neighborhoods, religious groups, unions and all sorts of small-scale social, civic, and political associations."

We can think of subsidiarity, says Fr. Andrew Greeley, as the principle of "no bigger than necessary."

In Keeping with North American Tradition

This principle of subsidiarity is a radical alternative to strains in our North American culture that, on one hand, put a premium on individual rights and, on the other hand, look to government to solve all social problems. Yet the subsidiarity or mediating structures approach has a long tradition in our country.

Contrary to "the popular image of solitary hero-figures," explains historian David Fischer, the American Revolution is a story about small, grass roots organizations. For example, "Paul Revere and the other messengers did not spread the alarm merely by knocking on individual farmhouse doors. They also awakened the institutions of New England." With "sustained planning and careful organization," the revolutionaries enlisted churches, family networks, and voluntary associations. Paul Revere himself belonged to five clubs or lodges in the Boston area. Samuel Adams belonged to the North Caucus, the Long Room Club, and more. The same is true of the others.

No wonder that, at the conclusion of his 1832 tour of the United States, Alexis de Tocqueville was left with a strong contrast between the North American and European ways of getting things done.

Americans of all ages, all stations in life, and all types of disposition are forever forming associations. There are not only commercial and industrial associations in which all take part, but others of a thousand different types—religious, moral, serious, futile, very general and very limited, immensely large and very minute. Americans combine to give fêtes, found seminaries, build churches, distribute books, and send missionaries to the antipodes. Hospitals, prisons, and schools take shape that way. Finally, if they want to proclaim a truth or propagate some feeling by the encouragement of a great example, they form an association. In every case, at the head of any new undertaking in the United States you are sure to find an association, where in France you would find the government or in England some territorial magnate.

A French visitor more recent than de Tocqueville made the same observation about our country. In the United States, said Jacques Maritain, there is "a swarming multiplicity of particular communities—self organized groupings, associations, unions, sodalities, vocational or religious brotherhoods, in which [people] join forces with one another at an elementary level of their everyday concerns and interests."

It is true that the rugged individual is a staple on the North American cultural landscape. Movies, novels, and legends pay homage to the self-sufficient detective, cowboy, or entrepreneur. It is also true, at the other extreme, that government plays an increasing part in the daily life of each North American. From business regulations to social security, from taxes to airport security, the government is seemingly everywhere. Federal service programs, conceived in the 1930s to assist struggling families, are now so bureaucratic that they often bring more stress than relief. Even the once meaningful slogan, "It takes a village to raise a child," is now used by some politicians to mean "Here comes another government program."

Yet, says Michael Novak, the genius and the reality of the North American experiment is neither "trusting the individual" nor "leaving it to the state....The secret to the psychology of Americans is that they are neither individualists nor collectivists; their strong suit is association, and they freely organize themselves, cooperate, and work together in superb teamwork."

The principle of subsidiarity, as applied by Catholics and others, thus can counter the negative dimensions of both individualism and of impersonal bureaucracy.

Robert Putnam of Harvard University has amassed evidence that not only are voting rates in this country in decline but also "by almost every measure Americans' direct engagement in politics and government has fallen steadily and sharply over the last generation." In addition, membership rates in church groups, labor unions, parent-teacher associations, and other voluntary organizations are falling. This trend amounts to a loss of "social capital," Putnam concludes. Its repercussions seriously damage our society.

Putnam's argument caught the popular imagination when he reported that "more Americans are bowling today than ever before, but bowling in organized leagues has plummeted in the last decade or so." The image of the lonely bowler has since become emblematic of the decline in community.

Publicity around Putnam's research has given a lift to Amitai Etzioni's communitarian movement, to the mediating structures philosophy of Peter Berger and Fr. Richard J. Neuhaus, and to publications and institutes specializing in civil society.

For full-time Christians, the bowling alone or social capital or civil society discussion is an opportunity to reclaim the principle of subsidiarity. Guided by that principle—whether or not the term is ever used—Christians have long celebrated intermediate buffer groups like the ethnic club, the parish, the precinct, and the union local. In fact, participation in organic society is not optional. For a full-time Christian it is wrong to willingly and knowingly neglect responsibility to, for example, a parent-teacher association, a professional organization, or a labor union.

Interestingly, the charge that affinity for parochial institutions produces narrow-minded citizens has been proven quite wrong. Of course, some unions led mostly by Catholics have, in years past, put barriers between blacks and careers in the trades. Of course, a parish organization here and ethnic club there has led an anti-integration campaign. But viewed with a wider lens, North Americans raised in a secure parochial environment are affirmative on all minority rights and progressive on many social policies. As political philosophers have known, research is now showing that particularity in this country can often be a major support to effective tolerance.

Delivery of Human Services

Our nation is in the midst of a serious public policy debate: what level of government should be responsible for welfare, food stamps, unemployment and disability benefits, affordable housing programs, and the like? Should government even be the provider of last resort or should the distribution of food, clothing, and shelter be left to individual initiative in the free market and to private charity?

The debate is often polarized between those who champion the government and those who hail the market. Each side assumes that it is the amount of money spent on social programs that really matters. Conservatives say it is more responsible to demonstrate toughness. Liberals (those few still around) hold out for more compassion. Social policy is caught in a paradox because North Americans overwhelmingly accept the legitimacy of the New Deal and Great Society objectives while they harbor deep skepticism about the means to implement the goals. People expect something to be done for the homeless, the elderly, the unemployed, the infirm, the poor. At the same time people of all persuasions are tired of government spending for social programs. This opposition to the New Deal and Great Society style of social policy is alternately called the great tax revolt, the awakening of the silent majority, compassionate conservatism, neo-liberalism, the Contract with America, Personal Responsibility and Work Opportunity, or the Welfare-to-Work movement.

The paradox has prompted social policy thinkers and political leaders to search for a third way—something different from government bureaucracy, but something responsive to people's real needs. What they are discovering is what Peter Berger and Fr. Richard J. Neuhaus call mediating structures: "Those institutions standing between the individual in his [or her] private life and the large institutions of public life."

The mediating structures approach is intriguing because it suggests a way to assist the poor or disadvantaged without impeding their freedom. It has the potential of avoiding unaccountable bureaucratic delivery systems and mitigating dependency in those being helped. The key to this approach is to recognize that everything public is not necessarily governmental; public health does not have to be governmentally delivered medical care; public aid is a much broader concept than checks from the government.

Just like the mediating structures approach, the Catholic principle of subsidiarity gets past the market vs. government logjam by asking: how are human services being delivered? Subsidiarity appreciates that individual interests and social responsibility are not necessarily opposed to one another. Rejecting collectivism and individualism, subsidiarity finds an integrating dynamic in the very nature of society and human beings. Subsidiarity concludes that people best achieve their natural (and supernatural) perfection by participating in mediating structures: families, community organizations, professional associations, unions, churches, and all kinds of voluntary associations. It thus realizes that people make more effective use of services delivered through those associations than those that arrive from an impersonal bureaucracy.

It must be quickly and clearly stated that subsidiarity is not simply an argument for private ventures rather than public assistance. A handy outpost of a medical conglomerate can be as impersonal as a large public hospital. A true mediating structure must be organically linked to the lives of the people it is serving.

Nor is subsidiarity anti-state. Charles Bouchard, OP, of the Aquinas Institute of Theology, says that subsidiarity is not in itself pessimistic about government, nor does it "see government and politics as a restraint on the effects of original sin." St. Thomas Aquinas, no less, thought there would have been government even if Adam and Eve had not sinned because even in paradise people, as social beings, would need a way to care for the common good.

Nor is subsidiarity a mere endorsement of handing-off social services to the fifty states. To believe in subsidiarity, says Msgr. George Higgins, "is not to say, without a carload of qualifications, that government is best which governs least or that so-called big government is by definition a violation of subsidiarity."

The genius of subsidiarity is to pay attention to how people are treated, to focus on the relationship between the caregiver and the person in need. Subsidiarity insists that the delivery of services remains as close as possible to the people in need. In the examples to follow, government and voluntary organizations work together to meet specific challenges.

Applications of Subsidiarity

A blighted Detroit neighborhood is the scene for an intense experiment in the welfare-to-work movement. Called Project Zero, the goal is to get every welfare recipient into a job. The state subsidizes private companies to hire recipients from that specific neighborhood. The state pays for job training. The state pays for drug treatment. The state pays for additional social workers, for counseling, childcare, transportation, tools, and uniforms—whatever it takes. The results have been quite mixed.

The towns of Grand Haven and Holland, Michigan, also committed to a Project Zero, getting every able-bodied welfare recipient into a job. This time, however, the social service officials contacted 250 churches and synagogues asking for volunteer doctors, lawyers, mentors, and sympathetic employers. Parishioners from St. Patrick's Parish and from Hardewyk Reformed Christian Church, for example, were matched with welfare recipients. The volunteers provided references, housing, auto repair, and fellowship for the recipients. Within a few months, those towns became the first in the nation to have no welfare recipients.

In a series about the welfare-to-work movement, the *New York Times* concludes that large, public workfare programs are not effective. On the other hand, small, private programs—often affiliated with churches—are reasonably successful in moving people from welfare into steady employment. Note, this is not an argument for turning all social problems over to the churches. In fact, were government to get out of the human service business, churches would quickly become over-extended and the needy would be inadequately served. Remember, the average inner-city congregation has fewer than 200 members and a total budget of less than $150,000. The average age of an inner-city pastor is fifty (higher if only Catholic pastors are counted).

In the Holland, Michigan, example the churches gave an assist to the rightful responsibility of the state. The churches made it possible for job training to be effective. The example, of course, raises many questions: should the government compensate churches for tackling social problems? Legally, how so? Should every church form a parallel, non-profit development corporation? What is to prevent church-based social programs from becoming bureaucratic? How much "religion" is allowed in a church-based social program that is related to a governmental department? Who monitors effectiveness?

Despite the impending controversies involved in these questions, there is increasing evidence that neither handing money or vouchers directly to individual clients nor surrounding those clients with government-administered programs is effective. As a stimulant to educational achievement, for example, government extracurricular programs—with the exception of some preschool efforts—have only minimal impact. The best predictor of success is the amount of social capital a student brings to class—capital accumulated by the student's parents or guardians as, over a lifetime, they make connections with neighbors, relatives, fellow parishioners, and coworkers by their participation in a mediating structure.

The principle of subsidiarity has something to offer many of the public policy issues of the day: housing, care for the elderly, immigration reform, education, and more. (It can also, of course, be creatively adapted to issues in business.) When it comes to day care policy, to take one more example, some favor a tax credit approach, allowing parents to spend the money any way they want. Others favor government funds, administered by the states, for licensed day care facilities that meet national standards. Both approaches overlook the possibility that a group closer to the working parents can probably deliver day care in a way that empowers the parents, even allowing—now this is heresy to both liberals and free marketers—the parents to spend less time on the job and more time at home.

Some political leaders in Europe, the United States, and recently even in South America, claim to be seeking an alternative to rugged capitalism and bureaucratic socialism. They have been using the phrase "third way" to describe their search. The same phrase, in the same context, has long been associated with Christian social thought and the principle of subsidiarity.

Christian social thought, John Paul II reminds us, is not in an ideological sense "a third way between liberal capitalism and Marxist collectivism." It is an approach, a way of looking at things. It is a tool that can be creatively adapted by Christians in all kinds of political, economic, and cultural settings.

Still, the search for alternatives is crucial. That politicians and public policy experts are discovering subsidiarity is an example of society discovering something the church often underappreciates. Perhaps in the months and years ahead full-time Christians, drawing upon the principle of subsidiarity, will offer creative and effective alternatives in public policy, business, healthcare, education, and civic life.

7

Family Life

> At all times and places...Christian families give priceless testimony to Christ before the world by remaining faithful to the gospel.
>
> —*Decree on the Apostolate of the Laity*

Christian social thought asserts that the family is not servile to society. Rather, society and the state are created to serve families. The family is a mediating structure between the individual and mega-institutions. It both forms a person to carry values into the wider world and buffers the individual from impersonal forces in that world.

The relationship between family life and North American culture is often cast as an either/or conflict, as in slogans like "the culture war" or the "the values war" or "the family under siege." Those catch phrases, however, have lately become overly identified with specific organizations, legislation, politicians, and preachers. The war metaphors also obscure the role that ordinary families play in creating and perpetuating the very culture that seems antagonistic to family life.

The relationship between the culture and family life is something like a river on which family life sometimes glides with positive cultural currents, but at other times must row harder against these currents. At all times family life must steer clear of dangerous objects, including those submerged below the surface of daily activity.

Many cultural currents that interact with family life could be discussed here—the drug culture, the therapeutic movement, the place of government programs, the multitude of abortions, the condition of public education, the propensity for litigation, and more. Instead, four representative cultural currents will be examined in detail—technology, fast food, the economy, and scheduling of children's activities. First, though, here is a review of two themes from Christian social thought, the mystical body of Christ and the communion of saints, as they relate to families navigating the culture.

The Mystical Body

In underscoring that God is really present in each person just as God is really present in the Eucharist, the doctrine of the mystical body of Christ reminds families that each person, irrespective of status, has inherent dignity. Therefore, family members are expected to extend respect to everyone they meet, especially "the least of these." Exposing youngsters to this concept of the mystical body is training in the virtue of solidarity, something essential for full-time Christians. The concept also suggests opportunities for full-time Christian families. Specifically, the mystical body is a reminder that in isolation one family or another has no chance of safely navigating the culture. The concept encourages a family to find support in the company of other families and to join with like-minded families in addressing the wider culture.

Just as with a physical body, the mystical body doctrine recognizes that, in associational life the decline of one type of mediating group is related to the decline of all others. Virtues are best inculcated through a flourishing of all social groups—families, clubs, precincts, unions, and the like. The strong individualistic current in our culture persistently slights this recommendation. Thus, for example, when men meet regularly in a Cursillo group to reflect on their marriage and family life, those men are bucking the dominant culture. When women regularly set aside a half-hour in their firm's conference room to support one another in their achievements at work and in the home, those women are creating a new cultural strain.

Jim and Kathy McGinnis of St. Louis, Missouri, are leaders in the Parenting for Peace and Justice movement. Through schools and churches, family members are invited to sign a pledge: "To respect myself…To apologize and make amends…To challenge violence in all its forms." Next, the family joins a few other families for discussion and support in a monthly circle of peace. From time to time the circle takes action in the community, perhaps circulating a petition to restrict hand-guns or sponsoring a dialogue with police representatives. The circle also networks nationally with the Families Against Violence Advocacy.

The McGinnis' model is similar to the Christian Family Movement that began in Chicago, in 1949. In CFM chapters, six to a dozen couples meet regularly to observe, judge, and act. That is, they use CFM materials to discuss some element of family life (observe); they weigh their experience against Scripture and Christian tradition (judge); and they resolve to make an improvement in their own family and in the neighborhood (act). At its peak over 150,000 couples belonged to CFM, a remarkable number considering that by design most young couples would stay with CFM for fewer than five years. The organiza-tion now maintains a national office in Ames, Iowa, although mem-bership has drastically declined since the early 1970s.

In his thorough history of the Christian Family Movement Jeffrey Burns points to problems of internal organization and conflicts with church teaching. It is, however, the strong strain of individualism in the wider culture that most accounts for the decline of CFM and other sim-ilar support movements for families, he concludes. Yet forums like CFM or Parenting for Peace and Justice, no matter how rare on today's scene, offer a valuable model with three crucial elements:

- a lightly structured gathering on a predictable basis;
- mutual support;
- modest action leading to reform both inside the home and in the community.

The Communion of Saints

The doctrine of the communion of saints reminds full-time Christians of the heavenly treasure house that is being administered by their ancestors in the faith. "The dead are [church] members in good stand-ing," explain Michael and Fr. Kenneth Himes. Those heavenly saints remain in communion with the living, who draw upon their good example and intercession.

The relationship with deceased relatives and other saints gives full-time Christians an opportunity to appropriate the best values of their parents, grandparents, and other models in the faith. The communion between heaven and the home starts as parents name their children after grandparents and other significant saints. It continues as parents use family stories—positive or negative—to convey lessons about education, work, and neighborliness.

Families participate in the communion of saints by retaining traditions, customs, expressions, blessings, and festivals from previous generations. Families share in the communion of saints by donating energy and money to unions, churches, or clubs that liberated their parents from the oppression or poverty of Europe and Latin America. Full-time Christian families honor the communion of saints by welcoming new immigrants and by eschewing any nativist politics.

The mystical body of Christ and the communion of saints are valuable "tools" for Christians as they negotiate the currents in our culture. Four of these currents, not necessarily more influential than others, deserve examination.

Technology Individuates

Christianity is generally positive about advancements in technology because Christianity understands that God is the ultimate author and engineer of all tools: books, maps, hospitals, laws, satellites, even the Internet. God created all the natural resources and built into each of them just the right degree of pliability necessary for their use by us. God, who created humankind, built into the human body and mind the ability to fabricate nature for good use. All tools are thus God's analogues which, when respected and used wisely, reveal something of the purpose or design of God.

On the other hand, Christianity is well aware that technology tends to distance people from each other. Even technologies that promise to link us often isolate us. The interstate highway system, for example, makes it possible to visit relatives 600 miles away in about ten and a half hours. But it was the interstate highway, along with other transportation and communication systems, that originally gave people the opportunity to take jobs in places that were far from home.

The telephone certainly helps people to stay in touch across the miles. But the telephone and its related technologies also encourage people in adjoining offices to communicate online rather than in person. Selwyn Becker, a professor at the University of Chicago School of Business, describes how he gets through a day using a cell phone and other technologies as a "socially acceptable way to avoid communication" with his wife, his children, his son's soccer coach, his secretary, and even his lunch companion. He is able to put each "sticky situation on indefinite hold" by taking a call or making a call. Sadly, some who hear of Becker's scheme don't realize he is being satirical.

The Internet certainly has the potential for putting people in contact with disparate friends, colleagues, and resources. Its users, however, are also dangerously isolated from their proximate siblings, school friends, and office mates, and even from themselves as they assume a fictional personality. A major study by Carnegie Mellon University, ironically funded by some of the biggest computer companies, concludes that mentally healthy people often become lonely after logging on into cyberspace. The Internet, the study concludes, is "building shallow relationships, leading to an overall decline in feelings of connection to other people."

Television, of course, is the technology that today most seriously isolates us. When, over thirty years ago, Jerry Mander presented arguments for the elimination of television, he readily admitted that most people would consider his proposal bizarre. Today, when daily home use of TV approaches eight hours and when nearly fifty percent of North American homes have more than three TV sets, Mander doesn't even get a fair hearing.

While people often consider TV to be a stress-reliever, there is growing evidence that TV increases daily pressure, lack of attentiveness, materialistic values, and spending. In fact, according Juliet Schor, "the more TV a person watches, the more he or she spends." Schor marshals evidence to counter the arguments that TV is an alternative to costly recreational spending and that TV does not promote consumer desire because its advertising is geared to low-cost items. Television, she argues, "inflates our sense of what's normal. [It] raises people's aspirations and leads them to buy more." Specifically, "each additional hour of TV in a week leads to an additional $208 of annual spending....Five extra hours a week raises yearly spending by about $1,000." A parent's TV hours are, as Schor also reports, inversely related to the amount of time spent with children but directly related to the amount of money that a parent spends on gifts for the children, including the latest videos.

In examining all the possible reasons why people are less involved in voluntary associations and civic life, Robert Putnam concludes that the single most significant variable is the amount of time spent watching TV. People are not disengaged because of increased pressures on the job or because of responsibilities to elderly relatives or several other more obvious explanations. It is simply because people prefer watching TV to participating in ethnic clubs or PTAs or church committees. "Each additional hour of TV viewing per day," Putnam estimates, "means roughly a ten percent reduction in most forms of civic activism."

Is there anything families, especially in a circle of support, can do to be countercultural regarding TV? Some families get involved in campaigns or intramural struggles to monitor the content of TV programs. These are noble fights. The bad consequences of TV, however, are only secondarily related to the type of program being broadcast or watched. The real culprit is simply time. The more hours spent in front of the television set, the less time and energy for reading, praying, interacting, exercising, joining civic groups, or even sleeping. The first and primary line of attack is to reduce the number of hours the television is on in the home.

Full-time Christian families, especially when they have the support of other families, try the following:

• They turn the TV on only to watch a specific program, not to "see what's on" or to have something going in the background.

• They turn the TV off after watching the desired program(s).

• They unplug the TV after each use.

• Each night they store the TV in a closet, even if its cart requires industrial size wheels.

• They throw away—not donate—one TV every year. (In most homes it takes three or four such losses before anyone notices.)

• They invest in any electrical or electronic devices—outlet covers, odd shaped plugs, a detachable antenna or products in design—that make the decision to turn on a TV more conscious.

• They temporarily give up the battle over TV content in favor of a battle against the quantity of TV.

Ritual Meals

Without ritual, people are emotionally and intellectually incapable of truly processing the most important moments in life. Without ritual, people naturally block out or treat casually the power and meaning of experiences like marriage, death, birth, or graduation. In contrast, ritual can be employed not only to digest the power of special occasions but also to appreciate the power of the seemingly ordinary. Thus, by conscientiously adding ritual to the family routine, the preciousness of daily life becomes more manifest.

Some time ago Oprah Winfrey challenged families to eat at least twelve meals together in a month. One of these families, the Swiss family of Baltimore, was featured on her television show and talked about how they met this challenge. This family of five—father, mother, and three children—was typically busy with work, school, and activities. Yet they were determined to meet the Oprah challenge even if it meant a 9:30 P.M. dinner one night and dinner in their station wagon parked in a school lot another night. The Swiss family learned some valuable lessons from the experiment—like, joked the mother, "don't eat chicken salad in the car."

There is a persistent theme in North American culture (shared by other cultures) that the family meal is as important to family life as fidelity is to marriage. Yet the family meal, like the family itself, is under threat—although things may not be as bad as suggested on *The Oprah Winfrey Show*. According to one survey, forty-five percent of North Americans said that "most of the family," although not all its members, ate together last night. On the other hand, the majority of those who said, "most of the family ate together last night," actually ate buffet style. In other words, the parents were in the kitchen or dining room while the children carried their food to another room. Further, about forty-two percent of the parents in the dining area were also watching TV. Likewise, the children were either watching TV, or using the phone or computer. The entire mealtime, by the way, was a half hour or less in sixty-eight percent of the situations.

The contours of the family meal have been shaped of late by changes in transportation and in the number of hours spent at work, as well as by the many activities in which family members engage. Another striking change is in the attitude toward restaurants. Of those who had a family meal last night, forty-eight percent ate in a restaurant or had takeout food. Each North American now averages four orders of french fries per week—a food item that is almost never prepared at home. During one ten-day promotional period in 1997, every North American child ages three to nine had on average four (count 'em...four) Happy Meals at McDonald's. In fact, the majority of all meals eaten by families are now prepared in a restaurant, with slightly over half of those restaurant meals eaten off premises.

The majority of today's restaurants are fast-food franchises where the goal is to have the food to the customer in fewer than three minutes. Five minutes is considered unacceptable in the industry. Two major restaurant chains tried to make fifty-five seconds the definition of fast, but a high turnover rate among staff, a large menu, and a high volume of customers at peak times temporarily put the goal out of reach. Some restaurant chains now equip regular customers with an electronic "speedpass" in order to shave seconds off the delivery time of their food.

The fast-food culture is a metaphor for family life where encounters are on the run and of predictable content. Why is it that families are so harried? Is it because of the substantial increase over the past thirty years in the number of hours women spend on the job? Is it because so many single mothers are raising families? Is it because of an increase in organized activities for children?

Statistics are not easily summarized. For example, are North American workers really putting in more hours at the office? On average, yes. But the word "average" can be misleading. There are, it turns out, at least two populations under consideration: the overworked and the underemployed. The breakpoint between the two categories falls at around forty-five hours a week. Those women and men who clock more than forty-five hours on the job are alarmingly increasing their work hours. Those others (hourly employees, part-timers, unemployed, the semi-retired) who clock fewer than forty-five hours a week are, on average, gradually decreasing time on the job in today's economy.

One thing seems certain: North Americans who want to process the meaning of daily life at the dinner table must now make a conscious, nearly countercultural effort to do so. Such families quickly forsake the idea of perfection. Not every member will be present—physically or emotionally—at every meal. Not every conversation will be uplifting, although some that are tense and argumentative might well be enriching. The bread is sometimes stale; the sauce is sometimes flat. Nonetheless, these countercultural families put a bottle of wine and a Bible on the table; they light a candle; they say grace; they break the bread. If the meal is eaten in a restaurant that doesn't serve wine or have candles, they simply say grace and break the bread. And oh yes, with no exceptions, they turn off the TV and the telephone. If necessary, they turn on the videocassette recorder and the answering machine during dinner.

It doesn't happen all at once, but with the ritual of wine, candle, bread, and grace the family meal gradually can become a sacrament of thanksgiving. Surprisingly, when conducted with a little ritual, some teenagers find the family meal, even with its arguments, to be as much fun as talking on the phone or hanging out. Many workers discover that ritualized family meals, with all their imperfections, are as stimulating as an hour in cyberspace or an extra hour at the office.

Stephen Covey, author of the popular "seven habits" books, says that many families, perhaps unable to pull off family meals, are conducting weekly meetings. The setting always includes food, either a full meal or snacks. The agenda is seldom heavy—although some serious topics can emerge—but encourages humor and stories. Yet, the occasion is called a "meeting" to establish a ritual. There might be an opening prayer. There might be a round of predictable questions with nondebatable answers: what are your true feelings this evening? What was your moment closest to Christ this week? What have you been reading?

Again, expectations for the family meeting or the family meal must be realistic. A modicum of arguing at the table, for example, is expected and can actually help everyone learn conflict resolution skills. (This is not the time for parents to interrogate their children, however.)

Putting ritual into the meal or other aspects of family life is not magic. Full-time Christians simply discover that over time rituals strengthen the family for whatever they do in the wider culture.

Family Wage

The marketplace is filled with ideas that support the priority of family life: on-site day care, family friendly work environments, maternity leave, job sharing, and more. As Arlie Russell Hochschild reports, however, these ideas are not being widely implemented, for a variety of reasons. Only ten percent of medium and large size firms actually offer child care benefits. Fewer than four percent of smaller companies offer any such benefits. In a well-known company with progressive policies, Hochschild found that a significant number of employees choose not to fully access the pro-family benefits. Many workers seemingly find more stimulation and satisfaction in a hectic workplace than in the normal pressures of home life. Either of free will or from perceived pressure, they stay on the job longer than required; they cut short paid maternity leaves; and they center their social life around work rather than exclusively around family.

The realities of the marketplace today are as follows: the disparity between the salary of top executives and all other workers is scandalously increasing. The gap between the wealth of the top five percent of all workers and the assets of the remaining ninety-five percent is widening. The purchasing power of working families is not keeping pace with the rising expense of healthcare, education, transportation, housing, and more. Consequently, the proportion of families with two primary wage earners or with one wage earner in two jobs is unprecedented and increasing. Finally, the number of women in the paid workforce is at an all-time high.

By contrast, the Christian social concept of a family wage envisions an economy in which a single salary is sufficient to meet a family's entire economic needs. This concept's original intention, however, is obscured amid one of the most prominent features of today's economy; that is, the large number of women bringing their talent to the marketplace.

By 1986 the United States Catholic bishops had dropped the phrase "family wage." Instead the bishops say,

Work with adequate pay for all who seek it is the primary means for achieving social justice....Society's institutions and policies should be structured so that mothers of young children are not forced by economic necessity to leave their children for jobs outside the home.

This language represents a nuanced shift from the United States bishops' statement of 1940:

The first claim of labor, which takes priority over any claim of the owners to profits, respects the right to a living [or family] wage. By the term living wage we understand a wage sufficient not merely for the decent support of the workingman himself but also of his family. A wage so low that it must be supplemented by the wage of wife and mother or by the children of the family before it can provide adequate food, clothing and shelter together with essential spiritual and cultural needs cannot be regarded as a living wage.

Furthermore a living wage means sufficient income to meet not merely the present necessities of life but those of unemployment, sickness, death and old age as well. In other words, a saving wage constitutes an essential part of the definition of a living wage.

The 1940 statement also contains a sentence that once was a hallowed plank in the social tradition: "It still remains true that a living wage constitutes the first charge on industry."

Writing in 1986, the bishops did not want to imply that the best model for family life is one in which one parent works outside the home while the other tends to homemaking full-time. The bishops face the fact that many women with children are in the workforce—either of necessity or because they enjoy bringing their talents to the marketplace. The United States Census Bureau reports that over sixty percent of women with one or more children under six years old are in the paid labor force. Of those mothers employed before the birth of their child, nearly eighty-five percent return to work before that child's first birthday. Thus Christian thinking on this topic is caught between a rock and a hard place. It wants to acknowledge the crucial role of mothering. At the same time it wants to endorse the opportunities now afforded women.

It thus requires some creativity to preserve the values contained in the old principle of family wage in today's economy. Thus, the bishops' fallback position is more and better day care. "For those children whose parents do work outside the home," they write, "there is a serious shortage of affordable, quality day care. Employers, governments, and private agencies need to improve both the availability and the quality of child care services."

Are there other ways, though, to retain the values of the family wage principle without adopting an antiquated model of family life?

The Business Executives for Economic Justice, a Christian group in Chicago, has developed livable wage guideposts for employers. For example, the BEEJ advises employers never to pay someone a wage that the employer would be unwilling to accept for the same job. The BEEJ also says that the first objective of a Christian business owner is not to receive the largest return on his or her investment of capital, talent, or time but to provide for the welfare of employees, suppliers, customers, and the community. The BEEJ concludes:

> A just wage refers to more than money. It reflects the stewardship of the manager who not only provides the prevailing market level compensation, but also a work environment that rewards production and encourages the individual to achieve and advance; respects everyone as an individual and encourages intellectual contributions...and provides sufficient health care.

Implicit in the BEEJ position is the Christian notion that a wage— any wage—is never equal to the value of work. "Precisely because work participates in the ongoing work of the creator," writes Helen Alford, OP, and Michael Naughton, OSB, no "wage, salary, perk, or benefit can [adequately] define the meaning of human activity."

The values of the family wage or living wage principle can also be bolstered by government policies. About seventy countries have what is called a family allowance; that is, a monthly government payment for each child in a household regardless of the income level, regardless if the mother is or is not employed outside the home. In many countries the family allowance is tax-free. In some countries the allowance is higher while the children are under three years of age and higher for any parent who is raising more than three children. The family allowance is not a welfare program for the poor. Indeed, a poor family might receive both welfare and the family allowance. It is not a substitute for a tax deduction, nor, as with the deduction for dependents in the United States, is its real value relative to a family's income.

The closest thing to a family allowance in the United States is the relatively new, modest child tax credit that is subtracted from what a parent owes on taxable income. The Earned Income Tax Credit, enacted in 1985, somewhat achieves the same desired purpose. President Ronald Reagan once called the EITC "the best antipoverty, the best pro-family, the best job creation measure to come out of Congress." It's complicated, but by way of example, a one-child family earning $12,200 gets a credit of, let's say, $2,257. If that family owes less than $2,257 in taxes, they get a check for the difference. A family qualifies for an earned income tax credit, depending on the number of children, until their income exceeds about $26,000.

Another idea making the rounds is to allow all parents to collect up to three years of social security at any time, to be repaid in one of several fashions upon retirement. The repayment, at least in one proposal, will be waived if the parent does not work outside the home during the years she or he takes the early social security payments. One more idea is to allow any parent who remains at home with a child under age three to collect unemployment insurance or receive a tax credit equal to half the national median income.

Each of these policies must be carefully debated. They and others like them, however, underscore the value of children as a major societal resource, and they enforce the obligation the whole society shares in the cost of rearing children. Lumped together, policies like continuation of the child tax credit, vouchers for day care and after-school programs, an increase in the minimum wage, and improvements in public education are part of a package necessary for a less stressed, more whole and holy family life.

Full-time Christian families, in consort with other families, advocate for pro-family economic and social policies at the voting booth, through their professional association, union, or precinct organization, and through other political means.

Action, Not Reaction

Over-scheduling, especially children's activities, is the bane of many a parent. It begins with the positive impulse to assist a child's physical, emotional, intellectual, and social development. It ends with countless trips to the regional soccer match, the accelerated tutoring session, the guidance counselor's office, and the martial arts studio.

This propensity to over-schedule is, in part, related to parents' insecurity in the face of what John McKnight calls "the professional invasion of the family." The invasion metaphor should not imply that coaches, counselors, and tutors are bad people. In fact, many over-scheduled parents are themselves employed in the helping professions, rendering service to other over-scheduled families. McKnight is trying to illustrate how children's needs are too often exclusively cast as individual deficiencies rather than in an economic or political context. Our service economy depends on a steady supply of physical, emotional, and educational needs. Thus, such an economy, by its nature, keeps raising the standards: children need more and more medical, psychological, physical, and educational attention. Each family, then, over-schedules in order to keep up with other families, who, in turn, keep pace with rising expectations.

Christians could look at our service economy, says McKnight, and "celebrate the institutionalization of the good servant. Ours is finally a society of caring, helping, curing servanthood." Unfortunately, servanthood that is delivered with commerce and a degree of control can quickly become lordship. McKnight wonders if Jesus, in his Last Supper discourse, had this problem in mind when he said: "I no longer call you servants...I call you friends."

Jesus' new emphasis on friendship suggests a way back from the tyranny of over-scheduling. Families, supported by circles of friends, are capable of admitting that a child's development is only marginally improved by outside activities and is, in fact, potentially damaged by too many activities. The best predicator of a child's academic success and future happiness, research now shows, is that child's intellectual and social capital—goods obtained inside the home and through a family's network of friends.

Family Life First, under the leadership of William Doherty of the

University of Minnesota, is a movement that seeks to temper the stress families experience as their children get involved in sports leagues and after school programs. The group, organized by local chapters, asks sports leagues, extracurricular programs, and youth groups in a particular area to sign a charter promising not to bench a child for missing a practice or two and not to schedule events on Sunday morning, among other things. The group then asks coaches and teachers to sign a pledge that the development of a child is more important than winning the tournament. After some negotiation, the local Family Life First chapter bestows its seal of approval on a given league or school program.

As Family Life First has discovered, change comes partially from the improved policies of the leagues or schools. More significantly, change occurs simply because like-minded parents meet other concerned parents through the Family Life First campaign. Strengthened by the mutual support found in the group, parents are able to tone down their own family's activity level.

The same dynamic occurs in other ways. As parents join a book discussion club or a workplace safety committee, they often improve the quality of life inside the home because they expose their children to more intellectual and social capital. Of course, there are people who attend community meetings as a way to avoid issues inside the home. A person who is, for example, hyperactive in parish functions can be a person with an unresolved personal life. On the whole, however, family life will not improve if each family merely tends to its own garden. Changes in culture and society require family members to participate in pro-family organizations or movements. It is there that families find the support and build the power to affect, rather than simply react to, the wider culture.

According to Doherty, the decline in genuine community involvement lies at the heart of a weakened family structure. The wider culture, he explains, puts the highest expectations on family life "but provides the least guidance as to how to achieve success." In fact, the culture undermines the family by draining it of energy. Most North American families are, he says, sapped by "time demands outside the home and electronic technology inside the home."

An entropic family is defined by Doherty as one in which individual members may have active lives but there is little energy for family life itself. He says that people today are consumed by activities but deprived of rituals that renew their energy. The pattern is reversed, Doherty concludes, only when family life becomes intentional—both within the home and as intentional families connect with other families to counteract the isolation of the wider culture.

A Politics of Generativity

The communion of saints, the mystical body of Christ, and indeed the entire Christian social framework connects families—past and present—to one another. It also orients full-time Christian families toward the future. Families influence our future by practicing what Robert Bellah calls "a politics of generativity." We are to care not only for people and things around us, says Bellah, but also to "endow our children and our children's children" with a worthwhile world. For starters, Bellah urges families to address the environmental crisis, to improve the treatment of children everywhere, and to temper the disparity between the rich and the poor.

Families swim through some curious currents. Celebrities and sports figures, no matter how tarnished, are routinely passed off as role models. Popular films and TV programs are replete with anti-heroes. Meanwhile parents are, at best, seen as noble chauffeurs and tireless cheerleaders. At worst, parents are blamed for all social problems involving children. According to a survey by the Public Agenda Foundation, nearly fifty percent of North Americans say "irresponsible parents," not social or economic factors, are the cause of juvenile delinquency. Only twenty-three percent feel parents are good role models for their children. In such a culture how refreshing it would be for children to accompany their parents to a pro-life rally, to a local food pantry, to a well-conducted union meeting, or to the voting booth.

Families that practice a politics of generativity, Bellah is convinced, create "a new moral paradigm—a paradigm of cultivation—[to] replace the old, outworn individualist one." For full-time Christian families, this approach is an investment in the future, precisely as they now make "social inclusion and participation" key themes in their life together.

8

The Common Good

The common good embraces the sum of those conditions of
social life by which individuals, families and groups can achieve
their fulfillment in a relatively thorough and ready way.

—*Pastoral Constitution on the Church in the Modern World*

There are many things in life that people can purchase with their own
money or obtain through their own ambition: theater tickets, a suburban home, a job promotion. There are other goods, however, that can
only be obtained by cooperating with others: neighborhood safety,
world peace, a clean environment, public health, and the like. A private good, explain Helen Alford and Michael Naughton, is something
that is owned by one person. Like a pizza, it can be shared with other
people only by dividing it. A common good, by contrast, can be
shared but not divided. A common good is shared as people participate in it.

The principle of common good points to the concern Christians
should have for the cooperative behavior and the communal structures
that produce good things like clean air, healthy surroundings, available
healthcare, accountable politics, fair laws, meaningful jobs, world
peace, and more. Actually, the concept of common good also reminds
people that even so-called private goods cannot be obtained without
the cooperation of hundreds of people routinely acting through well-
functioning markets, companies, organizations, and other institutions.
Out of respect for the common good, Christians are responsible for oil-
ing social machinery even as they go about their normal tasks.

The common good can be considered an ethical principle that goes beyond the utilitarian ethics so dominant in business and contemporary philosophy. It is not enough, says the common good, to maximize benefits for the greatest number of people or to base moral decisions on a cost-benefit analysis, no matter how sophisticated. An ethic that contains the principle of the common good sees a fallacy in maximum liberty philosophies, even as qualified by John Stuart Mill, John Rawls, or others.

The language of the common good offers an alternative to the language of the market. In a book titled *Everything for Sale*, Robert Kuttner writes that the market is the dominant metaphor for framing a wide range of activity, including education, the law, politics, the arts, even family life. The prevailing assumption is "that nearly everything can be understood as a market and that markets optimize outcomes."

Kuttner acknowledges that while the market is often a liberating force, "many forms of human motivation cannot be reduced to the market model." The current crisis in healthcare, for example, is a consequence of using only marketplace assumptions in an area that is premised on extra-market values. Sanitation, vaccination, nutrition, adequate housing, and other similar measures to prevent the spread of disease serve the common good interest of all, whether the direct beneficiaries of these measures can pay for them or not. Even when the provision of basic public health cannot be argued on the basis of enlightened self-interest, the common good insists on a free flow of values like compassion. Market forces, as Kuttner puts it, are an adequate way to deny luxury items to some people. But a good society must have enough non-market compassion so that people do not die simply because they cannot afford medical treatment.

In his bestselling studies sociologist Robert Bellah provides many examples of the prevalent language and assumptions from the marketplace. In an interview Bellah mentions the startling self-description by a bishop as "the CEO of the diocese." His priests are his "middle managers" and lay people are his "customers." Apparently this bishop believes that Christianity travels in one direction, from the professional service providers to the beneficiaries. This same market mentality has spilled over into family life with phrases like "quality time," "allocation of resources," "scheduling play time," "enrolling children in a competitive school," and "managing priorities." At a recent conference for college administrators, students were referred to as "consumers of our product." Colleges have to "bid for student talent" because "star value" in the student body affects the university"s "brand value."

In contrast, the common good does not believe that an unfettered market and individual calculus will eventually produce the best results for all. Instead, the common good pictures society like an organism with interdependent parts. While tradeoffs have to be constantly made, the common good warns that each piece of society, each piece of a family, each sector of a city is priceless. Each society is organically alive and therefore is greater than the sum of its parts. It is not enough, according to the common good, for parents to get their own children into a competitive school. Those parents must be concerned about reforming the school system. Nor is it enough for people to be occasionally generous to, for example, families who can't afford a competitive school or a first-rate nursing home. Full-time Christians and others of good will must routinely sacrifice for the sake of the common good. They must likewise design a good society in which "the least of these" obtain quality education, adequate healthcare, and other basic entitlements.

The core Christian message is about sacrifice, even unto death, yielding abundant life. In the same way, the common good asserts that acting with regard to the greater social good does not diminish one's personality. Full-time Christians who preferentially opt for the common good will gain "their fulfillment in a relatively thorough and ready way."

Solidarity

Solidarity is a companion to the common good. As a personal virtue, solidarity refers to the habits of heart and mind that compel Christians to take a wide view of the human condition and to sustain that view over the long haul.

From time to time high school students, college students, and young adults get involved in an "urban plunge," in AmeriCorps or the Peace Corps or the Jesuit Volunteer Corps, with Habitat for Humanity or with other service projects. Especially when combined with a reflection process, these experiences are incomparable. Volunteer projects during the formative years unlock the imagination and the capacity for a lifestyle that goes beyond the self and beyond the tribe.

Service projects agitate young adults, pulling them out of comfort zones and forcing them to develop a new vision. This happens, first, because the young adult volunteer is put to work with other volunteers who are strangers until then: students from other schools, adults, senior citizens, and others. Secondly, the volunteers serve people who come from family situations or neighborhoods or cultures that are often very different from their own. Through these cross-tribal connections, young adults develop empathy and broader patterns of thought that can grow into a lifelong determination to advance the common good.

As a social principle, solidarity provides the countervailing forces that are necessary to keep markets and governments accountable— trade unions, environmental groups, community organizations, and other associations.

It is no coincidence that the Polish dissidents of the late 1970s and 1980s, many of whom were steeped in Catholic social thought, chose the name Solidarnosc (Solidarity) for their freedom movement. According to the Catholic view there are false assumptions in a total government ideology as practiced in Poland during the Communist era, just as there are in a pure market ideology. Individuals, including so-called benevolent rulers, acting with the best intentions will inevitably harm other individuals if they simply pursue their own agenda or economic advantage. What is needed are countervailing groups—strangers who come together in common cause to form a membrane between free persons and the impersonal forces of government and the marketplace.

The principle of solidarity (sometimes called participation) reminds each mediating association—union, block club, precinct organization, professional association—to continually renew its aspirations lest it become as unaccountable as the bigger forces it is meant to buffer. Yet no society will be complete without such countervailing forces in which strangers come together and experience solidarity as they work for the common good.

Strangers around the Altar

In addition to participation in volunteer settings and civic organizations, Christians at the eucharistic banquet participate in an act of solidarity par excellence. The theme of solidarity or the common good is contained in the Latin word for banquet, *convivium*—literally, to live along with. The eucharistic banquet then, when celebrated fully, is an exercise in conviviality, in public solidarity.

A parish in Illinois has a standard epigraph at the top of each page in its bulletin. The one on page four says: "There are no strangers here." The saying is obviously meant to convey hospitality, and indeed that page of the bulletin usually announces social events in the parish. It is safe to assume that the parish certainly does not exclude strangers from participating at Mass. One would hope, however, that this parish and all others appreciate that many worshippers will properly remain strangers to one another after Mass.

The theme of church as community, which has enriched Christian life in the years since Vatican II, is underlined in the liturgy as worshippers sing as one chorus, as they pray the Our Father (especially when worshippers hold hands), as they exchange greetings at the Sign of Peace, and as they receive communion. The theme can, however, be misinterpreted.

Parker Palmer explains that God frequently speaks to us in public with "unique and compelling" words that cannot be heard "in the private realm." Drawing upon biblical examples, Palmer further observes that "the key figure in public life is the stranger." Abraham, to start near the beginning, is called out from his birthplace, his comfort zone, to found the religions of monotheism among strangers. It is strangers who bring Abraham and Sarah the promise of a son, strangers whom Abraham "runs to meet." It is a stranger who walks up to the disciples on the road to Emmaus, a stranger whom they invite into their home in that village. And there is this provocative line in Hebrews: "Remember always to welcome strangers, for by doing this, some people have entertained angels without knowing it."

"The idea of community is vital," says Palmer, and it is not opposed to openness to strangers. But, he warns, the theme of community or church as family can easily be romanticized. The church is not intended to be an experience of intimacy that precludes conflict, criticism, strangeness, problems of power, and compromise.

To complement the image of church as family, Palmer suggests church as school or church as halfway house. The image of church as campaign headquarters has also been proposed. Or accent the notion of church as family, Palmer says, but leave off the sentimental and include in the image feuding siblings, power plays in the family, the necessary shadow side of marriage, and the like. The point is to have an image of church that not only nourishes but also propels, a church that prepares its members for full public involvement, for public encounter with God.

Any act that helps people recall the common good in the midst of strangeness is religious in a sense. The eucharistic liturgy is certainly such an activity. During Mass, Christians touch the hands of strangers in the pew, share from a common loaf of broken bread, and drink from a common cup in solidarity with fellow worshippers—both those at that Mass and all those who go to Mass around the world.

Notice how many of the biblical incidents alluding to the Eucharist make the point that the meal is shared by peaceful strangers, irrespective of the diners standing with the government or in the marketplace. It should not be expected that people leave the eucharistic meal as intimate friends who agree on everything. Full-time Christians come away from the Eucharist knowing that, just as inside the church building, Christ resides in all the other strangers they will encounter during the week as they go about the task of promoting the common good.

In Praise of Compromise

In the minds of some Christians there are only two ways of making a decision: on the basis of a principle or with a lack of principles. The concept of the common good suggests a third alternative: make decisions by weighing conflicting claims, then compromise and act for the common good. This third alternative is not the same as reducing ethics to the lowest common denominator. Nor is it the same as majority rule.

There are some college students who have a global vision and a passion for justice. Here's an example: a few years back, students at several colleges became aware that the clothing bearing their school logo was manufactured in overseas sweatshops employing children. Using the latest technology to research the issue and old fashioned flyers to publicize their findings, these students brought their concerns to the attention of fellow students, teachers, administrators, and trustees.

But what were they to do next? Agree to majority rule? Most students, if allowed to vote, probably would have favored the status quo. Reach the lowest common denominator? Maybe everyone would settle for an innocuous sign in the campus store: "Warning. Some clothes are made in sweatshops." Neither majority rule nor consensus, it would seem, would have done much in this case to stem child labor.

To accomplish real change, the whole issue needed to be put into the context of the common good. The first step into that arena required pressure on the North American distributors of the clothing to impose new policies on their overseas contractors. But to get into a relationship with a major clothing company, the students needed allies, like the trustees of their college.

Here is where some sophistication was necessary on the part of the students. In order to engage the trust of the trustees, the students had to step away from the assumption that the trustees were totally lacking in principle because they allowed sweatshop clothing to be sold on campus. The trustees, for their part, had to let go of the principle that honorable students should never have blockaded the campus store or forcibly occupied the president's office—which the students had indeed done as part of their initial protest. Both sides needed to be willing to compromise in order to achieve their goal.

And so with allies like the trustees, other sympathetic business people, foundation executives, politicians, and union leaders, the students were able to come to the table with several major clothing companies. The critical lesson, which the students grasped, is that standing on high principle does less to alleviate child labor than does strategically exercising the virtue of compromise. Principle certainly has its place. In fact, people lacking principles are not even capable of compromise because their word doesn't extend beyond immediate experience.

It is also true that symbolic, principled protest is often necessary to awaken consciences. But it is a violation of the common good to insist on the best and squander the opportunity to accomplish the possible. Fr. Andrew Greeley puts it in strong words:

What is superior in pure theory is not necessarily and inevitably superior in the complex, ambiguous, and uncertain world of reality....The skilled compromiser is the most moral of [people] while the intransient ideologue is the most immoral.

Full-time Christians are reasonably comfortable with the reality that the common good is advanced compromise by compromise, messy detail by detail. Such Christians, in integrating faith with daily life, continually clarify their own motives, even as they admit that the right thing is sometimes accomplished for a so-called wrong reason and sometimes with the help of people whose private virtue is questionable.

Full-time Christians are in the habit of looking at choices through the lens of the public good, understanding that power and compromise can be highly ethical concepts. A full-time Christian, allergic to injustice, is adept at handling ambiguity, realizing that perfection is often the enemy of the good.

The Relational Individual

In the minds of some Christians there are two types of people: the selfish and the altruistic. The concept of the common good suggests a third category: the relational individual. Selfishness is obviously antithetical to Christianity. On the other hand, Christians are not exhorted to always act altruistically, giving no regard for the self. In fact, in most social circumstances pure altruism is not the most responsible course of action.

A father who selfishly spends twenty hours a week at the country club puts his job, marriage, and family in jeopardy. At the other extreme, a father who altruistically spends twenty hours a week volunteering at a food pantry also jeopardizes his job, marriage, and family. By considering the common good, a father will place his own interests in the context of his relationships with family members, coworkers, and the wider society.

The common good, please note, allows for some individual interest. Actually, it is difficult to image how someone could effectively advance the common good without a healthy sense of self-regard or, under one definition, of self-interest.

The problem is definition. In classical liberalism the word "individualism" means that the self is supreme and should be unencumbered by any constraints except to respect the opportunity for all other individuals to be similarly unrestrained. To a sensitive Christian, individualism in this classic sense sounds like selfishness. Nonetheless, in a culture in which liberty is a foundational theme, a case must be made for some type of individualism as an ingredient of spirituality. For if not, it might as well be admitted that a spiritual life on this continent is impossible.

Granted, Christianity must be somewhat countercultural. Yet Christianity also must be sympathetic to each culture, to each place where it intends to flourish. If Christianity gives wholesale condemnation or dismissal to the strong strain of individualism in North American culture, it is consigned to irrelevance. (This is also the case when Christianity wholeheartedly embraces North American individualism, and it becomes indistinguishable from the culture and separate from the true gospel.)

Close observers of North American culture are not so quick to put our understanding of individualism in a classical context, or equate it with selfishness. For example, in his famous essay in 1831 about the United States, Alexis de Tocqueville notes that individualism on these shores does not seem to be hard, selfish egoism so much as concern for one's own backyard. John Dewey, in a series of essays for *The New Republic* in 1929, points to a new type of individuality for our day— one that helps people to integrate the private and the public, to experience work as a contribution to the whole and as an instrument of culture, to be uplifted spiritually and to sense loyalty to particular communities and society at large.

Barry Alan Shain in a book titled *The Myth of American Individualism*, argues that neither the founders of the United States nor this country's influential Protestant ethic promoted a concept of liberty that champions "autonomous individual freedom or self-expression." Instead, North American individualism actually nurtures communalism. Even sociologist Robert Bellah and his colleagues, in books generally pessimistic about North American culture, note the "different languages of individualism," distinguishing selfishness from "expressive individualism."

How then to proceed? The concept of the common good concentrates on realistic behavior. It recognizes that most Christians, most of the time, act in a moral area somewhere between selfishness and altruism. In that middle area people must consider their own interests in relation to the interests of others, both short-term and long-term interests, both proximate and longer-range consequences. To simply set self-interest in opposition to the general welfare is, as Reinhold Niebuhr explains, "to ignore nine-tenths of the ethical issues that confront the consciences of [people]."

The mix of self-interest with the needs of others is implied in this quotation from Rabbi Hillel, as found in the Mishnah: "If I am not for myself, who will be with me? If I am only for myself, what am I?"

Today's busy Christians, it would then seem, need guideposts along a road to holiness that winds around the twists and bends of proper interest for oneself in the context of regard for others. Unfortunately, guideposts for realistic Christians are rarely presented in homilies or in adult catechesis. In rightful condemnation of selfishness and in pleas for additional charity, many preachers and religious teachers seem to denigrate all material interests and all types of self-interest.

The challenge is to find ways to celebrate the moral formation of a person who recognizes that true self-regard actually pushes the self into regard for others, and that selfish behavior actually diminishes self-regard. This is not an easy prospect in our culture, overripe with materialism and selfish individualism. The only way, however, to significantly advance the common good in such a climate is to build on the legitimate ambitions and self-regard of responsible people. Full-time Christians are relational individuals; that is, they cherish liberty and individual rights but they also relish community and responsibility.

Private Property

The right of private ownership is one of the most precious rights asserted in North America. It is also quite compatible with the notion of the common good.

Long before the failure of communism, the philosophy of the common good posited that private property is an antidote to collectivisms, totalitarianisms, dictatorships, and other oppressive systems. Pope Leo

XIII's encyclical *Rerum Novarum*, for example, marshaled arguments in defense of private property to counter the thinking of Karl Marx and other nineteenth-century reformers who regarded private property as the original sin of social systems. The insight of Leo XIII is that people are more likely to exercise responsibility for the common good when they are secure with their own individual property than when most property is collectively held.

Back in 1891, however, Leo XIII had in mind a small farm as the model for ownership—and appropriately so. But owning and managing forty or 400 acres of farmland is one thing, owning 400 shares of stock is another. The difficulty in applying Christian teaching on ownership is that the nature of private property keeps evolving into new shapes and forms. By 1961 Pope John XXIII was well aware that conditions of ownership were changing from physical things to investments when he wrote in *Mater et Magistra*:

> It is quite clear today that the number of persons is increasing who, because of recent advances in insurance programs and various systems of social security, are able to look to the future with tranquility. This sort of tranquility was previously rooted in the ownership of [a farm or residential] property.

In the new context, the *responsibility* of private ownership, rather than the *right* to private ownership, is often a more pressing ethical matter. Pope John Paul II aptly expresses this side of the coin: "There is a social mortgage on all private property." In other words, Christians must be alert to how even their private property is serving the common good.

In that regard it is interesting to note, with management guru Peter Drucker, that through their pension funds and other investments ordinary workers now hold at least two-thirds of the equity capital and perhaps fifty percent of the debt capital in the North American economy. This observation is not to minimize the scandal of the widening wealth gap in North America. It serves, however, to highlight the moral responsibility that accompanies investments in mutual funds, selected stocks, savings accounts, IRAs, and other retirement funds.

As yet, there are only inadequate socially responsible investment tools. Social responsibility is further handicapped because workers do not always have control over their investments, particularly the massive pension funds. Lately, some people have gotten involved in their union or professional association precisely to gain better control over where pension funds are invested. Because of such involvement, some pension funds now invest only in stocks associated with companies acceptable to the workers. For example, a union pension fund would not own shares in an anti-union company. Under a similar mindset, some public employee pension groups have lobbied specific corporations in which they own shares for improvements in company policy.

Most religious orders and judicatories, as stewards of donations given by ordinary Christians, apply some moral criteria to their selection of investment tools. Many, particularly through the Interfaith Center on Corporate Responsibility in New York City, lobby companies in which they own stock.

The strategy whereby religious groups reform corporations through stockholder resolutions was pioneered in March 1967. FIGHT, a black community organization in Rochester, New York, affiliated with Saul Alinsky's Industrial Areas Foundation, was embroiled in a protracted struggle with Eastman Kodak Corporation over minority hiring and promotion. FIGHT bought some shares of Kodak stock, and it also asked religious groups around the world holding Kodak shares to assign FIGHT as a proxy voter at the annual shareholders meeting. The drama surrounding that meeting, with FIGHT leaders waving their stock proxies, led to job training programs cooperatively managed by FIGHT and Kodak.

From time to time the Industrial Areas Foundation has employed a similar greenlining tactic on a parish level. For example, people in one or more parishes sign a pledge to move all their savings accounts and IRAs to the one bank that does the most for mortgage availability in that area. The banks then actually compete to attract new homeowners, instead of discouraging young families from buying in a so-called redlined or bad neighborhood.

Sophisticated campaigns like this, in which parishioners pledge to invest or shop with the one bank, insurance company, or supermarket that does the most for the common good has, it seems, great potential for addressing neighborhood blight, parochial school finances, health-care delivery, and the like. The entire question of responsible investment is really something new for Christians, and it awaits the creativity of today's young adults.

9

Characteristics of Incarnational Christians

By his incarnation the Son of God has united himself with every person. He worked with human hands, thought with a human mind, acted by human choice, and loved with a human heart.

—*Pastoral Constitution on the Church in the Modern World*

Ron Krietemeyer of the Office for Social Justice in St. Paul, Minnesota, knows some full-time Christians who are committed to transforming our messy world and finding holiness in so doing. He calls such people "incarnational Christians." It might follow that certain behaviors or characteristics are common to such people.

Incarnational Christians are constantly sought out and confronted by God in the midst of life's hustle and bustle—not away from it. Correspondingly, it is a religious duty for incarnational Christians to attend to the signs of God's presence in everyday life, for—in the words of Vatican II— "nothing genuinely human fails to raise an echo in the hearts of the followers of Christ."

Incarnational Christians are sensitive to the sacred potential in what appears to be mundane human experience in their work, leisure and neighborliness, worship, acts of citizenship, preaching, catechesis, and social action. Incarnational Christians know that embedded in the ordinary lies the extraordinary, the miraculous, the salvific, the holy.

Incarnational Christians are assisted by pastors and other church ministers who recognize that the exchange of love between God and God's people is mediated through our grace-filled, created world—just as God's love is present through the Sunday Eucharist.

Incarnational Christians are sure contemplation or reflection is a prerequisite for thoughtful action. Incarnational spirituality, however, turns toward the world. For incarnational Christians the path of salvation and the life of the whole church course through the experience of parents, students, workers, neighbors, friends, and spouses.

Incarnational Christianity rests on the truth that God so loved the world that God became a baby in a trough, a carpenter, a common criminal on a cross, a human being—a coworker in an office, a neighbor, a machinist, a customer, a middle-manager, a nurse, an accountant, a spouse. Through the redemptive love of Christ we are called to make our lives a little sacrament...raised up, broken and blessed... bread of and for the people we meet on the job, around the home, and in the neighborhood.

Incarnational Christians intuitively sense that the best apostles in a given situation are usually those Christians closest to the situation. The proper and important role of parents, technicians, reporters, bankers and janitors should be respected, their gifts acknowledged, and their competency cultivated and utilized.

Incarnational Christians are eager to gather with like-minded Christians and others to transform the world. Without hesitation, each baptized person must take the initiative. Mature Christian women and men do not wait for programs emanating from a rectory or diocesan agency in order to shoulder their responsibility in the world. Today's incarnational Christians gladly cooperate with priests, religious, and other church employees in advancing the faith in the home, the neighborhood, and the marketplace.

Concerted Action

Incarnational Christians, as Ron Krietemeyer observes, are pragmatic. They sometimes settle for better when perfect is not attainable. They are also pluralists, not purists. That is, they take initiative on an interfaith basis whenever possible. In fact, they realize that reform is not normally obtained by explicitly invoking religious language. Therefore, incarnational Christians do not have to examine the religious credentials of people who are struggling for the common good. As pluralists, incarnational Christians can comfortably work well with people on specific programs, even while knowing that those people do not agree with them on everything.

Incarnational Christians look to their respective denominations to support them in their own religious tradition while at the same time encouraging their members to join with their neighbors, coworkers, and colleagues to humanize social, political, and cultural institutions.

Incarnational Christians hold human wisdom in high esteem and discard any type of fundamentalism coming from the right or the left. Incarnational Christians pray the Scripture each day but they do not exclusively turn to the Bible (or to episcopal pronouncements) for solutions to problems in the home, the community, or on the job. They realize that, taken literally, the slogan "What Would Jesus Do?" is usually worthless.

While incarnational Christians are confident that faith belongs in public life, they are offended when the gospel is invoked in support of a political ideology or specific public policy. Except in a few cases, incarnational Christians are skeptical when church professionals, armed with an encyclical or a Scripture passage, seem to know the Christian position on a thorny social issue.

Instead, incarnational Christians bring the truth of revelation to bear on specific problems through the prism of their experience, imagination, and reason. They read the newspaper and articles in sociology, political science, medicine, management, and more with the same religious conviction as they read the Bible. Stranded on a deserted island with only one book, incarnational Christians might very well prefer *The Practical Guide to Shipbuilding* over the Bible.

Incarnational Christians, while believing that God is quite capable of miracles, sense that God is quietly energizing and participating in the world through the design or processes God implants in stars, planets, minerals, genes, cells, institutions, and human beings. Incarnational Christians thus feel honored to gradually discover the one Truth by way of physics, biology, chemistry, psychology, management, art, history, political science, and medicine.

Incarnational Christians, while sensitive to excessive individualism and materialism in our culture, appreciate that positive spiritual impulses have always moved across and through the North American continent. The North American experience—with its history of immigration, its praxis of mediating institutions, its respect for diversity within unity, its freedom of religious expression, and its arts of negotiation and conflict resolution—is consistent with Christianity and, as such, affords an opportunity for theological reflection in order to deepen Christian wisdom. At the same time, incarnational Christians know that wherever North American culture falls short of the city of God, they have a duty to raise human consciousness and direct the culture toward the common good.

Incarnational Christians think of themselves as citizens, not as taxpayers. They understand that the formation of citizenship is a top priority for the whole church, without which the church grievously betrays its mission. Incarnational Christians are on the lookout for forums in which they can learn more about social virtues and their application to daily life on the job, around the home and in the neighborhood. In particular, incarnational Christians seek tools for understanding how they are often manipulated by evil in their culture and by mediocre institutions.

Incarnational Christians respect the healthy urge for inner peace. They believe, however, that a genuine spirituality cannot neglect the virtue of social justice, the exercise of which may be emotionally disturbing. Incarnational Christians get involved, not waiting until each person has inner peace or until everyone is in consensus. Incarnational Christians are aware that those people who, for example, marched in Selma, Alabama, for the cause of civil rights had imperfections. But according to incarnational spirituality, souls are partially changed simply by marching. By the same theology, incarnational Christians do not shy away from less-than-perfect community organizations, political machines, trade unions, or professional associations.

The Sanctity of Work

Contrary to a message sometimes prominent in the Christian tradition, incarnational Christians believe work is participation in God's ongoing creation and in Christ's redemption. Good work is a way women and men, individually and collectively, offer their best to the earthly city and to the city of God. Work itself is capable of contributing to the spiritual life.

Incarnational Christians are sensitive to inhumane working conditions, unethical business practices, unresponsive social structures, and other blemishes on the plan of God. They are, nonetheless, very optimistic about what is developing in technology, science, industry, construction, commerce, the arts, and other areas of human endeavor. They perceive a strong affinity between openness to the future and Christian hope.

Incarnational Christians are appreciative of courses, publications, and associations dedicated to business, legal, or medical ethics. More so, they are attracted to forums that help them grapple—not simply with ethics—but, in the words of Vatican II, with "the meaning of all this feverish activity."

Incarnational Christians have a simple faith. They believe that people do God's will on the job, as well as within their families and in their neighborhoods, when they act with love, justice, integrity, and care.

Incarnational Christians are offended when, in broad strokes, the legal profession, electoral politics, or business are dismissed as unChristian. Though their faith is simple, incarnational Christians are seasoned enough in the real world to resist simplistic sloganeering—positive or negative—about family life, business, and politics.

Incarnational Christians admire people whose careers involve teaching the untutored, caring for the sick, or preaching the gospel. But they know a vocation in God's world is not confined to those who, as the expression goes, work for the good of humanity. How well one works, how one seeks just relationships at work, and what one does with one's work generally define the value of work.

Workaday Christians know that God's kingdom advances incrementally. They do not apologize for the small steps they take toward advancing peace, alleviating poverty, and enhancing human dignity. Foreign missionaries and the like certainly promote the kingdom of God, but so do conscientious carpenters, homemakers, artists, executives, janitors, and editors.

Incarnational Christians donate money to church agencies toward the salaries of people whose full-time work is to transform society. Incarnational Christians know, however, that giving flesh to gospel values from inside their own workplaces, businesses, schools, and communities is the crucial work of justice and peace.

Wholeness and Holiness

More than ever before, incarnational Christians live by the injunction "Keep holy the sabbath." They are convinced that an economy that encourages workaholics is no friend to incarnational spirituality. They are crafting an economy and a culture that value holiness (wholeness), one that provides for a sabbath day each week, some sabbath minutes each day and, optimally, a sabbath retreat once a year.

Incarnational Christians are responsive to the announcements at Mass for involvement in parish committees and neighborhood organizations. They quietly realize, however, that the most responsible activity for a busy Christian on a given evening or Saturday morning may well be to nourish his or her family life, intellectual life, or cultural life.

Incarnational Christians support a living wage as every person's birthright. But equally important are music, literature, and beauty. Incarnational Christians are, as Vatican II says, "conscious that they are the artisans and authors of the culture in their community" and thus they strive to nurture the best in the arts and society.

Incarnational Christians are aware that the mission to bring about God's kingdom on earth as it is in heaven belongs to them because of their baptism. Incarnational Christians are the church in the heart of the world and bring the heart of the church to the world.

The word "vocation" and the vocation crisis, incarnational Christians insist, are not restricted to the ordained priesthood, the permanent diaconate, or vowed religious life. There is a shortage of people answering the call to be committed citizens, responsible parents, dedicated teachers, compassionate nurses, and more. There are crises in the vocations of parenting, management, engineering, exploration, research, and more.

Incarnational Christians expect parishes, Newman Centers, and all church agencies to evaluate their programs in the context of how well those programs train and support the baptized to live the gospel on the job, around the home, and in the neighborhood. All of the courses and programs used to train the laity for church ministry—either as volunteers or as professionals—need to be evaluated against their effectiveness in focusing the lay ministers on the crucial task of inspiring other baptized people for their work in the world.

Full-time Christians

Incarnational Christians are intrigued by the years Jesus spent in obscurity. That is, they appreciate that Jesus' creative and redemptive mission included his time as a student, a carpenter, a son, a friend. Incarnational Christians live Jesus' gospel through their own work as students, carpenters, neighbors, and family members.

Further, incarnational Christians believe that their active style of faith has the potential to bring meaning and peace to our troubled world. This is not, incarnational Christians know, a simple proposition. It requires disciplined study and reflection. It requires humility and a distaste for religious triumphalism. It requires pro-active openness to others, including Jews, Muslims, and people of all backgrounds and faiths.

Incarnational Christians in this new century realize that the stakes are high. Yet, in partnership with like-minded people, they are eager to act in the world. They have discovered an abiding joy in being full-time Christians.

Appendix

A Chicago Declaration of Christian Concern

The signers of this Declaration are members of the Catholic community in Chicago.

For decades, the church in Chicago nurtured a compelling vision of lay Christians in society. The vision was eventually accepted and celebrated by the Second Vatican Council. That same vision produced national movements and networks that generated a dynamic lay leadership. It attracted priests and religious who saw their ministry as arousing the laity to the pursuit of justice and freedom; who served the laity without manipulating them.

Shall we passively accept that period of history as completely over, and with it the vision that proved to be so creative? While many in the church exhaust their energies arguing internal issues, albeit important ones, such as the ordination of women and a married clergy, the laity who spend most of their time and energy in the professional and occupational world appear to have been deserted.

"Without a vision the people shall perish." Who now sustains lay persons as they meet the daily challenges of their job and profession— the arena in which questions of justice and peace are really located? Where are the movements and organizations supporting the young toward a Christian maturity? Where are the priests [and other church professionals] sufficiently self-assured in their own identity and faith that they can devote themselves to energizing leaders committed to reforming the structures of society?

We wait impatiently for a new prophecy, a new word that can once again stir people to see the grandeur of the Christian vision for society and move priests [and other church professionals] to galvanize people in their secular-religious role.

We think that this new prophecy should retrieve, at least in part, the best insights of Vatican II. It was Vatican II that broadened our understanding of the church. It rejected the notion that church is to be identified exclusively with hierarchical roles—such as bishop and priest. The church is as present to the world in the ordinary roles of Christians as it is in the ecclesiastical roles of bishop and priest, though the styles of each differ.

Vatican II identified hopes for social justice and world peace with the church's saving mission. The salvation of the world is no longer to be construed as applying only to individual persons but embraces all the institutions of society. The church is present to the world in the striving of the laity to transform the world of political, economic, and social institutions. The clergy [and other church professionals] minister so that the laity will exercise their family, neighborly, and occupational roles mindful of their Christian responsibility. The thrust of Vatican II is unmistakable:

> What specifically characterizes the laity is their secular nature. It is true that those in holy orders can at times be engaged in secular activities, and even have a secular profession. But they are, by reason of their particular vocation, especially and professedly ordained to the sacred ministry. Similarly, by their state in life, religious give splendid and striking testimony that the world can not be transformed and offered to God without the spirit of the beatitudes. But the laity, by their special vocation, seek the kingdom of God by engaging in temporal affairs and by ordering them according to the plan of God. They live in the world, that is, in each and in all of the secular professions and occupations. They live in the ordinary circumstances of family and social life, from which the very web of their existence is woven. Today they are called by God, that by exercising their proper function, and led by the spirit of the Gospel, they may work for the sanctification of the world from within as a leaven. In this way they may make Christ known to others, especially by the testimony of a life resplendent in faith, hope, and charity. Therefore, since they are tightly bound up in all types of temporal affairs, it is their special

task to order and to throw light upon those affairs in such a way
that they may be made and grow according to Christ to the praise
of the creator and redeemer.

—*Dogmatic Constitution on the Church, #31*

Although the teaching of Vatican II on the ministry of the laity is
forceful and represents one of the Council's most notable achievements, in recent years it seems to have all but vanished from the consciousness and agendas of many sectors within the church.

It is our experience that a wholesome and significant movement
within the church—the involvement of lay people in many church
ministries—has led to a devaluation of the unique ministry of lay
women and men [in the world]. The tendency has been to see lay ministry as involvement in some church related activity, e.g. religious education, pastoral care for the sick and elderly, or readers in church on
Sunday. Thus lay ministry is seen as participation in work traditional-
ly assigned to priests or religious.

We recognize the new opportunities opened up to men to become
permanent deacons, but believe that in the long run such programs
will be a disaster if they create the impression that only in such fashion do the laity mainly participate in the mission of the church. We
note that our misgivings are shared by the Apostolic Delegate to the
U.S., Archbishop Jean Jadot, who commented recently: "I believe in
the laity. And the laity as laity. I was very, very impressed, I must say,
by my experiences in Africa and my closeness and friendliness with
some African bishops who don't want to hear about a permanent diaconate. They say it will kill the laity in the church. It will kill the laity
in the church because it will reinforce the conviction already existing
that to work for the church you must be ordained."

Our own reaction to the 1976 Detroit Call To Action conference
reflects a similar ambivalence. Without a doubt, it was historic, prece-
dent-setting in its conception, in its consultative process, in helping all
levels of the church listen to each other and in facing challenges to
growth affecting the inner life of the church. But devoting, as it did, so
much of its time to the internal affairs of the church, the conference
did not sufficiently illuminate the broader mission of the church to the

world and the indispensable role of lay Christians in carrying out that mission.

During the last decade especially, many priests [and other church professionals] have acted as if the primary responsibility in the church for uprooting injustice, ending wars and defending human rights rested with them. As a result they bypassed the laity to pursue social causes on their own rather than enabling lay Christians to shoulder their own responsibility. These priests and religious have sought to impose their own agendas for the world upon the laity. Indeed, if in the past the church has suffered from a clericalism on the right, it may now face the threat of a revived clericalism—on the left.

We also note with concern the steady depreciation, during the past decade, of the ordinary social roles through which the laity serve and act upon the world. The impression is often created that one can work for justice and peace only by stepping outside of these ordinary roles as a business person, as a mayor, as a factory worker, as a professional in the State Department, or as an active union member and thus that one can change the system only as an outsider to the society and the system.

Such ideas clearly depart from the mainstream of Catholic social thought which regards the advance of social justice as essentially the service performed within one's professional and occupational milieu. The almost exclusive preoccupation with the role of the outsider as the model for social action can only distract the laity from the apostolic potential that lies at the core of their professional and occupational lives.

Although we do not hold them up as models adequate to present-day needs, we do note with regret the decline and, too often, the demise of those organizations and networks of the recent past whose task it was to inspire and support Christians in their vocation to the world through their professional and occupational lives. We have in mind such organizations as the National Catholic Social Action Conference, the National Conference of Christian Employers and Managers, the Association of Catholic Trade Unionists, the National Council of Catholic Nurses, Young Christian Students, Young Christian Workers, and the Catholic Council on Working Life.

Although concerns for justice and peace are now built into church bureaucracy more so than when such organizations flourished, there is no evidence that such bureaucratization has led to further involvement of lay Christians. As a matter of fact, the disappearance of organizations like the above, and our failure to replace them, may have resulted in the loss of a generation of Catholic leadership.

As various secular ideologies—including communism, socialism, and liberalism—each in turn fail to live up to their promise to transform radically the human condition, some Christians seek to convert religion and the Gospel itself into another political ideology. Although we also yearn for a new heaven and a new earth, we insist that the Gospel of Jesus Christ by itself reveals no political or economic program to bring this about. Direct appeals to the Gospel in order to justify specific solutions to social problems, whether domestic or international, are really a betrayal of the Gospel. The Good News calling for peace, justice, and freedom needs to be mediated through the prism of experience, political wisdom, and technical expertise. Christian social thought is a sophisticated body of social wisdom which attempts such mediation, supplying the middle ground between the Gospel on the one hand and the concrete decisions that Christians make on their own responsibility in their everyday life.

In conclusion, we address these words of hope and of deep concern to the members of the church throughout the nation as well as to members of the church in Chicago. We invite them to associate themselves with this Declaration. We prayerfully anticipate that our words and theirs will prompt a re-examination of present tendencies in the church and that out of such a re-examination will emerge a new sense of direction, a new agenda.

In the last analysis, the church speaks to and acts upon the world through her laity. Without a dynamic laity conscious of its personal ministry to the world, the church, in effect, does not speak or act. No amount of social action by priests and religious can ever be an adequate substitute for enhancing lay responsibility. The absence of lay initiative can only take us down the road to clericalism. We are deeply concerned that so little energy is devoted to encouraging and arousing lay responsibility for the world. The church must constantly be reformed, but we fear that the almost obsessive preoccupation with the church's structures and processes has diverted attention from the essential question: reform for what purpose? It would be one of the great ironies of history if the era of Vatican II which opened the windows of the church to the world were to close with a church turned in upon itself.

—*Third Sunday of the Coming of the Lord, 1977*

Original signers and their titles in 1977:

Russell Barta, professor of sociology, Mundelein College

Albert J. Belanger, Alliance of Catholic Laity

Cecelia Brocken, associate dean, College of Health Sciences, Rush University

Martin J. Burns, attorney

M. Josetta Butler, RSM, past president, St. Xavier College

Morris Bohannon, service analysis officer, US Postal Service

Msgr. Daniel M. Cantwell, pastor, St. Clotilde Parish

Alcuin Coyle, OFM, president, Catholic Theological Union

Patty Crowley, co-founder of Christian Family Movement

Agnes Cunningham, SSCM, president, Catholic Theological Society of America

Dorothy A. Drain, religion editor, *Chicago Defender*

Susan Durburg, psychiatric nursing consultant, Evanston Hospital

Fr. James Finno, associate pastor, St. Mary Parish, Evanston, IL

Fr. John E. Flavin, president, presbyterial senate of the Archdiocese of Chicago

Fr. Vincent Giese, Our Lady of Perpetual Help Church

Fr. Raymond E. Goedert, pastor, St. Barnabas Parish

Patrick E. Gorman, chairman of the board, Amalgamated Meat Cutters and Butchers

Robert F. Harvanek, SJ, professor of philosophy, Loyola University

Carol Frances Jegen, BVM, professor of religious studies, Mundelein College

Bishop King, assistant to superintendent for minority groups, Archdiocese of Chicago schools

Thaddeus L. Kowalski, president, Polish American Congress, Illinois Division

George Leighton, judge, United States District Court, Northern District of Illinois

Franklin McMahon, artist / reporter

Irene Leahy McMahon, writer/ homemaker

Ed Marciniak, president, Institute of Urban Life; chair, Center for Urban Ethnic Affairs

Eugene P. Moats, president, Local 25, Service Employees International Union

Samuel W. Nolan, deputy superintendent, Chicago Police Department

Edward J. Noonan, architect; president of Chicago Associates

Robert Olmstead, reporter

John Pawlikowski, OSM, associate professor, Catholic Theological Union

Faustin A. Pipal, chairman of the board, St. Paul Federal Savings & Loan

Jorge Prieto, M.D, chairman, department of family medicine, Cook County Hospital

Luz-Maria Prieto, director, Mujeres Latinas en Accion

Lawrence Ragan, editor, *The Ragan Report*

Bruce Rattenbury, director of public relations, Rush Presbyterian-St. Luke Medical

Jolyn H. Robichaux, president, Baldwin Ice Cream Co.

Edmund J. Rooney, reporter, Chicago *Daily News*

Mary Schiltz, project associate, Institute of Urban Life

Don Servatius, president, Local 165, International Brotherhood of Electrical Workers

Fr. John Shea, instructor in systematic theology, St. Mary of the Lake Seminary

Carroll Stuhlmueller, OP, president-elect, Catholic Biblical Association
of America

Lawrence J. Suffredin, attorney

William H. Tate, chairman of the board, CCT Press, Ltd.

Dan Tucker, member of the editorial board, *Chicago Tribune*

Fr. Thomas Ventura, chairman, Association of Chicago Priests

Fr. John J. Wall, instructor in theology, Niles College, Loyola
University

Anne Zimmerman, executive administrator, Illinois Nurses'
Association

References

A Chicago Declaration of Christian Concern. National Center for the Laity, PO Box 291102, Chicago, IL 60629.

Alford, Helen, OP and Michael Naughton, OSB. *Managing As If Faith Mattered: Christian Social Principles in the Modern Organization.* Notre Dame, IN: University of Notre Dame Press, 2001.

Bellah, Robert. *Individualism and Commitment in American Life: Readings on the Theme.* New York: Harper & Row, 1987.

Bellah, Robert, et al. *The Good Society.* New York: Vintage Books, 1991.

———. *Habits of the Heart: Individualism and Commitment in American Life.* Berkeley, CA: University of California Press, 1985.

"Interview with Robert Bellah." *Catholic Messenger*, February 20, 1997.

Berger, Peter and Richard J. Neuhaus. *To Empower People: From State to Civil Society.* Washington, DC: American Enterprise Institute, 1977, 1996.

Bernardin, Cardinal Joseph. "Let's Look at the Whole Vocation Problem." *Catholic New World*, January 7, 1983.

Brown, Robert McAfee. "The Church Today: A Response." *The Documents of Vatican II.* New York: America Press, 1966.

Burns, Jeffrey. *Disturbing the Peace: History of the Christian Family Movement 1949-1974.* Notre Dame, IN: University of Notre Dame Press, 1999.

Carey, Archbishop George. "Empowering Priesthood of All Believers." *Keep the Faith*, Fall 1993.

Covey, Stephen. *Seven Habits of Highly Effective Families.* New York: Golden Books, 1997.

de Tocqueville, Alexis. *Democracy in America.* New York: Doubleday and Co., 1969.

Dewey, John. *Individualism: Old and New.* New York: Capricorn Books, 1929.

Doherty, William. *The Intentional Family: Simple Rituals to Strengthen Familiy Ties.* Reading, MA: Addison-Wesley Publishing, 1997.

———. *Take Back Your Kids.* New York, NY: William Morrow & Co., 2000.

Drucker, Peter. *The Unseen Revolution: How Pension Fund Socialism Came To America.* New York: Harper & Row, 1976.

———. *Managing in Turbulent Times.* New York: Harper & Row, 1980.

Eberly, Don, editor. *The Essential Civil Society Reader.* Lanham, MD: Rowman & Littlefield Publishers, 2000.

Ferree, William. *The Act of Social Justice.* Washington, DC: Catholic University of America Press, 1942.

———. *Introduction to Social Justice.* Washington, DC: Center for Economic and Social Justice, 1997.

Fischer, David H. *Paul Revere's Ride.* New York: Oxford University Press, 1994.

Florman, Samuel. *The Civilized Engineer.* Boston: St. Martin's Press, 1987.

Geaney, Dennis. *Christians in a Changing World.* Chicago: Fides Publishers, 1959.

George, Cardinal Francis. "What the Church Brings to the Neighborhood." *Origins,* May 22, 1997.

Glendon, Mary Ann. "Beyond the Simple Market-State Dichotomy." *Origins,* May 9, 1996.

Greeley, Andrew. *Building Coalitions.* New York: Franklin Watts Inc., 1974.

———. *The Communal Catholic.* New York: Seabury Press, 1976.

———. *Neighborhood.* New York, NY: Seabury Press, 1977.

———. *No Bigger than Necessary.* New York: New American Library, 1977.

Häring, Bernard. "Lessons of a Lifetime." *America,* November 18, 1989.

Hecker, Isaac. *Sermons Preached at the Church of St. Paul the Apostle During the Year 1863.* New York: Arno Press, 1978.

Higgins, George. "The Social Mission of the Church after Vatican II." *America*, July 26, 1986.

——. "Subsidiarity in the Catholic Social Tradition: Yesterday, Today and Tomorrow." Albert Cardinal Meyer Lecture, University of St. Mary of the Lake, April 1994.

——. *World: Vatican II's Pastoral Constitution on the Church in the Modern World*. Chicago: Catholic Action Federations, 1967.

Himes, Michael and Kenneth Himes. *Fullness of Faith: The Public Significance of Theology*. Mahwah, NJ: Paulist Press, 1993.

Hochschild, Arlie Russell. *The Time Bind: When Work Becomes Home and Home Becomes Work*. New York: Henry Holt & Co., 1997.

John XXIII. "Mater et Magistra." *Seven Great Encyclicals*. William Gibbons, SJ, ed. Mahwah, NJ: Paulist Press, 1963.

John Paul II. *On Human Work*. Boston: Daughters of St. Paul, 1981.

——. *On Social Concern*. Boston: Daughters of St. Paul, 1987.

——. "Opening Address at the Puebla Conference." *Puebla and Beyond*. John Eagleson and Philip Scharper, eds. Maryknoll, NY: Orbis Books, 1979.

Kuttner, Robert. *Everything for Sale: The Virtues and Limits of Markets*. New York: Twentieth Century Fund, 1997.

Mander, Jerry. *Four Arguments for the Elimination of Television*. New York: William Morrow & Co., 1978.

Marciniak, Edward. "On the Condition of the Laity." *Challenge to the Laity*, edited by Russell Barta. Huntington, IN: Our Sunday Visitor Press, 1980.

——. *Reversing Urban Decline*. Chicago: Institute of Urban Life, 1981.

Maritain, Jacques. *Reflections on America*. New York, NY: Charles Scribner's Sons, 1958.

McCarraher, Eugene. "Smile When You Say Laity." *Commonweal*, September 12, 1997.

McKnight, John. *The Careless Society: Community and Its Counterfeits*. New York: Basic Books, 1995.

Merton, Thomas. *Life and Holiness*. New York: Doubleday Books, 1963.

Mill, John Stuart. *On Liberty*. Amherst, NY: Prometheus Books, 1859, 1992.

Murnion, Philip and Anne Wenzel. *The Crisis of the Church in the Inner City*. New York: National Pastoral Life Center, 1990.

Nagorski, Andrew. *The Birth of Freedom: Shaping Lives and Societies in the New Eastern Europe*. New York: Simon & Schuster, 1993.

National Conference of Catholic Bishops. *Economic Justice for All*. Washington, DC: US Catholic Conference Publishing, 1986.

————. "Statement on Church and Social Order." *Justice in the Marketplace*. Washington, DC: US Catholic Conference Publishing, 1985.

Niebuhr, Reinhold. *Love and Justice: Selections from the Shorter Writings*. Cleveland, OH: The World Publishing Co., 1957.

Norris, Kathleen. Interviews in *Hungry Mind Review*, Spring 1996 and December 1997.

Novak, Michael. "Mediating Institutions: the Communitarian Individual in America." *The Public Interest*, Summer, 1982.

Palmer, Parker. *The Company of Strangers*. New York: Crossroad Publishing Co., 1983.

Pierce, Gregory F.A. *Spirituality@Work: 10 ways to balance your life on-the-job*. Chicago: Loyola University Press, 2001.

————. *Activism That Makes Sense: Congregations and Community Organization*. Chicago: ACTA Publications, 1984.

Pius XI. "Quadragesimo Anno." *Seven Great Encyclicals*. William Gibbons, SJ, ed. Mahwah, NJ: Paulist Press, 1963.

Leo XIII. "Rerum Novarum." *Seven Great Encyclicals*. William Gibbons, SJ, ed. Mahwah, NJ: Paulist Press, 1963.

Putnam, Robert. *Bowling Alone: the Collapse and Revival of American Community*. New York: Simon & Schuster, 2000.

Rawls, John. *Theory of Justice*. Cambridge, MA: Belknap Press, 1971.

Sayers, Dorothy. *Creed or Chaos?* Manchester, NH: Sophia Institute Press, 1949.

Schlosser, Eric. *Fast Food Nation: The Dark Side of the All-American Meal*. Boston: Houghton Mifflin Co., 2001.

Schor, Juliet. *The Overspent American: Upscaling, Downshifting, and the New Consumer.* New York: Basic Books, 1998.

————. *The Overworked American: The Unexpected Decline of Leisure.* New York: Basic Books, 1991.

Schumacher, E.F. *Small Is Beautiful: Economics As If People Mattered.* New York: Perennial Library, 1973.

Shain, Barry Alan. *The Myth of American Individualism: The Protestant Origins of American Political Thought.* Princeton, NJ: Princeton University Press, 1994.

Woods, Robert. *The Neighborhood in Nation Building.* New York: Arno Press, 1923.

Of Related Interest

The Poor Are the Church
A Conversation with Father Joseph Wresinski,
founder of the Fourth World Movement
Gilles Anouil

We can only appreciate Christ if we fully understand him in terms of his decision to live as one of the poor. Fr. Wresinski tells us that to truly be the church, we must be in communion with the poor, share their suffering, understand that the poor are "us." A powerful and insightful challenge to all Christians.

1-58595-183-8, 240 pp, $16.95

Brave New Church
From Turmoil to Trust
William J. Bausch

Father Bill Bausch knows about parish life in the Catholic church firsthand. In this, his latest offering, he focuses on twelve challenges facing the church today. He then considers the transitions and responses that can move the church forward as it seeks to minister to parishioners of the twenty-first century. Father Bausch writes in a clear, informative, and uplifting style and he frames his arguments in a way that is both pastoral and incisive, shaping his ideas and suggestions with solid historical background and strong Catholic principles.

1-58595-135-8, 320 pp, $16.95 (J-85)

Catholic Social Teaching and Movements
Marvin Krier Mich

Putting human faces on the Church's social teachings: that's what this unique book is about. The author aims to tell the story of Catholic social tradition from the perspective of the official teachings and the movements and persons that expressed and shaped that teaching.

0-89622-936-X, 488 pp, $29.95 (J-06)

Available at religious bookstores or from:

TWENTY-THIRD PUBLICATIONS
A Division of Bayard PO BOX 180 · MYSTIC, CT 06355
1-800-321-0411 · FAX: 1-800-572-0788 · E-MAIL: ttpubs@aol.com
www.twentythirdpublications.com
Call for a free catalog